Juror Number One
and the
Alternate Retirement Plan

David M. Porter

For more information about the author, to order additional books or request information about speaking engagements, visit: DavidPorterBooks.com

Published by P&A Agency, LLC.

ISBN-10: 1536875198
ISBN-13: 978-1536875195

Dedication

To the love of my life, my wife, Lauren.

CONTENTS

ACKNOWLEDGMENTS

I could not have written this book without the help of an incredible number of people, too many to name them all.

My wife, Lauren, who loved me enough to encourage me to write this and then loaned me to the book writing process for months on end. You make me strive to always be a better man.

Dave and Virginia Porter, who raised me to be the man I am. Without you, I wouldn't be where I am today – literally. Your advice and direction set the course for my life. I'm *eternally* grateful.

Tony Jackson who gave me my first shot in the business and Dave Bryant II who told me it could be done, thank you both.

Jamie Parker who first set me on the path of the "Rich Man's Roth" – a business colleague who became my friend. A few lines in a book doesn't do justice to the help and friendship you've given me. Thank you.

Amit Berger, thank you for being a friend and business mentor. I appreciate you and our talks more than you know.

Joel Hamm, Andrew Jenkins, Greg Windham, Stacy Korsgaden and Chris Donaldson – thanks for your friendship and all the help along the way.

To all of the people who have been involved with this book – editing, proofreading, fact checking and encouraging, I thank you.

To everyone I have failed to name – Thank you!

CHAPTER 1
INTRODUCTION

When I started writing this book, I wanted the writing to be professional in manner. Retirement, investing, life insurance, fixed incomes, planning for the future in general, can be very heavy subject matter so I wanted to write this book with a light feel. Please don't misunderstand the light nature of the writing style for anything other than a serious look at an alternative to the 'normal' retirement plans available today.

I am a Christian. That might sound like a weird place to start a book about investments and retirement savings, but bear with me a second. You might not be a Christian. You might not like Christians or religions in general, but it plays a role that's directly related to you. As a Christian I am compelled to do what's best for others. My religion calls on me help the needy, to lend to the poor, to give of myself, to 'love my neighbor as myself,' to be honest and walk in integrity. If you were to look closely, you would see that I have character flaws just like everyone else. I'm human. I'm not perfect. But I do everything I can to live a life that is pleasing to my Savior, Jesus Christ. I'm writing this book in service of my Savior, trying to convey my thoughts in a manner that is pleasing in His eyes. What that means for you, if I do it correctly, is that this will be the best of everything I have. You'll be the recipient of a product done in service of my Savior, not a product done in service of my wallet or in service of my ego. I'm writing this for Him, not for me or you – we just get to be the beneficiaries of a product with a very high standard.

I need to go one step further with you. A brief family history - Both of my parents were police officers. My mother quit the police force when I was born and when she decided to go back to work, she started working for a church ministry. She's done that for over 30 years. My father retired as a police officer after almost 23 years and then went into the insurance profession where he spent another 25 years (so far) helping people protect their lives and their assets. My sister works in full-time ministry with by brother-in-law who is the pastor of a rapidly growing church. I come from a home where every member has dedicated their lives to helping people. It's all I've ever known.

Let me tell you a little about my Dad. He is the most genuine man I have ever known and this isn't just hero worship. He has lived a life of integrity and honesty and literally helped thousands and thousands of people. My goal in life, to this day, is to be *half* the man that my Dad is. If I can accomplish that one goal, I will be the most successful man in the world.

Why am I telling you about my family, about my dad? It explains one of the biggest reasons that I do what I do the way I do it. That reason is my name. My name is the most important thing I have. Proverbs 22:1 says "A good name is to be more desired than great wealth..." The reason my name is so important to me, is because it's not only my name. My father is named David Porter as well and I never, ever want to do anything to tarnish, hurt or disparage my Dad's name. My name is the most important thing my Dad has given me and therefore I do everything in my power to make sure I live up to it, that my business lives up to it, and that my staff live up to it.

So there you go. I tried to make all of that as short as possible so we could get to the real reason you're reading this book – the *Alternate Retirement Plan*.

CHAPTER 2
THE DEPOSITION

Holy Cow! That was exhausting and I've only just started.

"What exactly was exhausting?" you might be wondering, *"You've only typed two sentences... and I'm being pretty lenient giving 'Holy Cow' sentence status."*

I'll tell you and I promise, I'm not making any of this up. This is my first experience writing a book. I wasn't sure where to start, so I asked a friend who has published a handful of successful books, how he did it and if he could give me any pointers. Andrew, my friend, told me exactly how to do it and said if I had any questions along the way, he would be happy to help me in any way he could. Basically, he said step one (after you know what the subject matter was going to be) was to use this certain computer program and load the 'styles' that I wanted my fonts to look like for the content of the book - you know, the chapter headings, subtitles, body copy of the book, etc. He said once you've got that, just start typing away. He said I could do things like page breaks, start new chapters, or emphasize certain things and it would be easy to make changes along the way because once I set up the program, all I had to do was hit 'the button' and it would correct things in the entire book for me.

So getting back to what was exhausting, this is it - It took me an hour to *find the menu* to set up the 'styles' of this book. An hour. To find the menu.

"Why didn't you call your friend, Andrew, and ask him for help?" you're probably thinking to yourself right about now, right? Honestly, I was embarrassed about not being able to even start the book. I figured his help would be needed later and I didn't want to use up all of my *'phone-a-friend'* lifelines before I even really got going. I know Andrew would have been happy to help me, he's that kind of guy. I just wanted to do this on my own. If I'm being honest, I think 'just wanting to do this on my own,' will end up costing me down the line. I'm pretty sure, even now, I've done something incorrectly in the setup of this book and Andrew and I will be 'fixing' it later.

All of that got me to thinking and it dawned on me that this is a perfect metaphor for the way things work in our personal lives and in the 'real' world. There are some absolutely wonderful things that we can take advantage of, like Andrew's computer program knowledge, but we're too ashamed to ask the questions we need to or to show our vulnerability to someone who could help. We **know** that these people can help - whether it's starting on your first book, baking a birthday cake or looking for alternative ways to save for retirement. We think, *'I got this. I'll check Google. I'll look at Pinterest. I'll send out a 'silent' prayer request on Facebook and hope 'The Big Guy Upstairs' shows me the answer.'* Trust me. Sometimes, it's better to just ask someone who knows what they're doing. If you had seen my one and only birthday cake attempt, you'd understand where I'm coming from.

Well, I can't bake a birthday cake, I'm obviously not any good at this computer program (yet) and the jury is still out on if I can successfully write a book, but I do know one thing: I know what I'm doing when it comes to using the *Alternate Retirement Plan.* My goal, with Andrew's help, is to put that knowledge into book form.

So, let's pretend that you came to my office and asked me a question, something like *"I've invested in my company's sponsored 401k, but I'm afraid of the taxes that I'm going to have to pay and I'm afraid that I might run out of money after I retire. What else can I do?"* I'm going to go above and beyond your expectations and explain the *Alternate Retirement Plan* to you. No need to be embarrassed. No need to be ashamed. Consider this your inexhaustible 'phone-a-friend.'

There are some other, wonderful books about this *Alternate Retirement Plan* on the market today. I might even quote from some of them along the way. The problem I had as I was reading them is, because of the technical nature of the *Alternate Retirement Plan*, they are a little difficult to understand in certain places or concepts - and I'm a trained professional! I want to give you the knowledge that will help you going forward, but in a way that is easy to comprehend. You know, real people talk. Not lawyer talk. Not investment advisor talk. Not salesman talk.

I'm not trying to get rich here (people don't tend to get rich writing books about retirement plans). I genuinely just want to help people. I've had the opportunity to travel, I've been invited to speak in several different places about this *Alternate Retirement Plan* because people realize I have something of value locked inside my brain. I'm willing to make that knowledge available (it's not a secret!) - I just need a place to do it. This book is that place.

As I said, there are some wonderful books about

this *Alternate Retirement Plan* on the market today, but I want to approach this subject matter in a unique style and treat this book in a completely different manner than the other authors did. I am going to be presenting the *Alternate Retirement Plan* as though we were in a court of law. I am going to be presenting my case to you. I realize this *Alternate Retirement Plan* is so completely out-of-the-box that people sometimes have a hard time grasping the idea and the inner workings of it. Hopefully, if I've done my job well, it will answer all your questions.

Some final thoughts before we get into our 'court case' - I am not a tax professional (besides, in between the time I typed that sentence and the moment you read it, it's likely that the tax code has changed 15 times). There is no magic bullet when it comes to investments. The 'perfect' retirement solution for Mr. Client A, might be the **worst** possible solution for Mrs. Client B.

This might be one of the most important things you will read in this entire book. It's so important, I am going to **bold** the rest of the paragraph (that shows exactly how important I think it is. Do you know how long it took me to find the 'bold' button?). **If, after reading this book, a light bulb has flashed in your mind and you think this might be the perfect solution for you - GO SEE A PROFESSIONAL in your area. DO NOT try to work this *Alternate Retirement Plan* by yourself.**

If the professional that you speak with doesn't understand what you're talking about, buy a copy of this book and give it to him or her or go find another professional who knows what they are doing. This is your future we're talking about. Please don't go to someone who might do something incorrectly that could cost you hundreds of thousands or millions of dollars (yes, really) down the line. Please.

This book is not intended to give any tax or investment advice. It is not intended to make or suggest any personal recommendation as to what is most fitting for any specific individual. This book is solely intended to be informative and offer a new perspective on retirement planning. Hopefully, it will give you a few hours of enjoyable reading along the way. I repeat: Go see a knowledgeable professional in your area.

CHAPTER 3
THE COURT IS CALLED TO SESSION

Full disclosure here - I've never been to watch a trial in real life. I've never been involved in a court case. I wouldn't even know where to go to watch a live court case. The closest I have come to seeing a court case is on episodes of *Law and Order, Perry Mason, Matlock* and in John Grisham movies. In other words, I'm not a lawyer. I've never been to law school and everything I know about 'lawyering' was learned from television and pop culture. With that in mind, I invite you to 'go to court' with me right here, in this book.

I'm going to play the role of a much younger, Matlock-type, folksy, country lawyer (I'm from Alabama) and I'm going to invite you to play the role of unbiased *Juror Number One*. You can play

11

your role in any way you want - as a young city-slicker just starting a career, an immigrant with a dream, a single mom or dad, an established business owner, a rancher, a police officer or doctor or dentist. All I ask is that you play your character without bias. That's the important part. Be unbiased. Can you hear the *Matlock* theme music in your head?

When it comes to different methods of preparing for retirement, you probably have some preconceived ideas. You likely have heard different television or radio personalities speaking about retirement, life insurance and investing. You've probably done some internet research. All I ask is that you have an open mind. If you can't do that, if you can't be unbiased, you should probably put this book down right now and save yourself a couple hours. But, if you continue reading, you and I will have this agreement: I'll shoot straight with you, give you all the information I have as honestly and in as easily digestible bites as I can, and in return, you'll read with an unbiased view.

Why is it so important to be unbiased? Like I mentioned, you probably have some preconceived ideas about investing and saving for retirement. Sometimes people hear some of the terms I am going to talk about and think a certain thing because of their preconceived ideas - like a man holding a knife at a crime scene. He looks guilty!

He's got a knife! But what if those preconceived ideas are not completely correct? What if the man holding the knife just cut the ropes off the kidnap victim? Some of the terms you'll hear in this book will look familiar (like that guy holding a knife), but don't immediately jump to the conclusion that the terms are definitely what you think they are (a criminal). Rather, keep an open mind and see the terms for what they are (a man with a knife cutting the ropes off of your retirement savings).

Let's take this *Alternate Retirement Plan* and put it on trial. I move that this *Alternate Retirement Plan* is the most incredible, fantastic, money-making, money-retaining, retirement plan available today. I am going to play the lawyer 'proving' that point to you here, in this court today.

Now, if we were going to trial, there would be a few things that you would need to know before you made up your mind and declared a verdict. Remember, you're currently unbiased?

First, we have to know what we're talking about. In the opening statements of this case, I'm going to have to give you a lot of terms. I'm sorry. I'll try and keep it all as simple as possible, using metaphors along the way, but we have to be using the same terms and have the same definitions so that we are certain we are headed in the right direction, together.

Think of it this way, if I said "Look, a bear!" you might think I'm talking about a polar bear or grizzly bear. If my next sentence was something like "I can't wait to see my niece's face as she hugs it!" You'd think I was nuts! But that would be because you and I weren't thinking of the same kind of bear. I, obviously, was thinking of a *teddy* bear. While talking about this subject matter, we need to make sure we are both thinking of the same type of bear.

Second, you would need to know some background on this type of *Retirement Plan*. Where did we come from, how did we get here, and why is it important going forward? We will begin with the history of this *Alternate Retirement Plan* to know that we are both starting from a common point.

Third, you would want to see all of the evidence that would prove my point. Keep in mind I am trying to prove the case that this *Alternate Retirement Plan* is the most incredible, fantastic, money-making, money-retaining, retirement plan available today. Don't worry though, as the only 'lawyer' in this book, I'll do my best to show both sides of the case with anything that might considered a downside to the *Alternate Retirement Plan* listed in the "Circumstantial Evidence" category. There will be evidence shown for retirement plans in general and evidence shown for this specific *Alternate Retirement Plan.*

The judge presiding over this case has just walked into the courtroom. The bailiff booms, "All rise!"

Juror Number One, shall we begin our case?

CHAPTER 4
THE LAWYER BEGINS

Wow. One member? This is the smallest jury I've ever dealt with in my time as a lawyer. That's fine, though. It just means I only have to convince one person...

Opening Statements

Juror Number One let me begin the case by asking you this question: What would you think if I told you that I was going to give you a retirement product that would:

1. Capture market gains whenever they occur;
2. NEVER participate in market losses;
3. Lock in the money you earn each year, so you could never lose it;
4. Allow you to access your money, even your gains, tax free;

5. Allow you to access your money for any reason, at any time and at any age without penalty;
6. Allow you to keep your money invested for as long as you like without penalty;
7. Be protected if you're sued or involved in a lawsuit (depending on the laws of your state);
8. Provide a large, income-tax free, payment to the person of your choosing if you died prematurely;
9. Allow a portion to be accelerated for purposes of chronic illness, acting in the stead of long-term care (without charge until activated)?

You would probably think this sounds too good to be true, right?

Let me tell you about my cousin Joel. He is one of the smartest people and one of the most successful people I know. He has a business sense and a 'street' sense that are second to none. You know what I mean when I say street sense? He has a nose for when something (a product or an offer) smells good and when that something is rotten. He can find a way to make money or a way to pull someone out of trouble in the middle of seemingly any circumstance. Joel's told me for as long as I can remember, "If something sounds too good to be true, it *probably* is." It's one of his 'go-to' phrases, one of the standards he lives by. In that sentence though, there's one word I want to focus on. It's the word *'probably.'* 'Probably' leaves some measure of doubt – it could be possible or it might not be possible. It could be true or it might not be true. That's the power of probably.

In this particular instance, this product that *"probably"* sounds "too good" is *actually* true. Over the course of the next several pages, I'm going to prove it to you. One by one, step by step, we'll look at each of those nine statements. We'll dissect the nuances and we'll have a clear understanding of how each item can, without-a-doubt, be true. We'll also show how those nine items aren't found together in any other retirement vehicle available today – which makes this product, what I've deemed the *Alternate Retirement Plan*, the most incredible, fantastic, money-making, money-retaining, retirement plan available today. How incredible is it? Roughly 85% of the CEOs of Fortune 500 companies utilize some form of this *Alternate Retirement Plan.*

I recently sat down with a friend and client, Chris, and explained just a portion of the *Alternate Retirement Plan* to him. Now, Chris is a very successful business man and he couldn't understand why no one had explained this to him. The questions came in a flurry. *"Why haven't I heard of this before now? Is this true? When can I start? Why isn't everyone taking advantage of this? How can this possibly be true?!? Why doesn't the world know about this? What's the catch? Is this some sort of secret?"* he asked. He was beside himself.

The reality is it's not a secret. There is only a small percentage of people who have the correct licenses to be able to provide the *Alternate Retirement Plan*. Most of the professionals that help people plan and save for retirement – think employees at investment firms, bankers, accountants, lawyers, etc. – don't have all the licenses to provide this product. They might have *some* of the licenses, but not all of them. Since those investment firm employees, bankers, accountants, lawyers and the like, don't have the necessary licenses to provide this product to their clients, why then, would they recommend it? Legally, they can't. That's why it's so important to go to the right kind of professional when wanting to start your own *Alternate Retirement Plan*. Chris realized he had come to the right place. Don't worry. By the end of this court case, you'll be able to find the right professional as well.

Terms and Definitions

Now, *Juror Number One*, to begin to prove my case for the *Alternate Retirement Plan*, we need to get on the same page. So I'm going to give you some terms and definitions. I'm going to break them down as much as possible, but please remember, these definitions, analogies, metaphors and examples are for purposes of proving a point to you. These are not Webster's definitions. These are not legally binding definitions. These are David's definitions. In the world of finance, things are constantly changing and the way one retirement vehicle works today as I'm writing this, might not be the way it works, or might not have the same rules, when you're reading this. Keep that in mind as we run through these terms and definitions.

Retirement: The end goal. What we're all working towards. It's that magic time when all of our years of hard work are rewarded by being able to relax, spend time with family and friends, travel, see the world, maybe buy some toys – boat, sports car, or possibly a lake house. For many people it's a scary place that's looming in their future, coming like a tsunami – something they've never thought about, something they've never prepared for.

Investment capital: This can really mean a lot of different things, but in our court case, just think of it as your money. This is the money being used to help with your retirement. Another way of saying it is, this is the money (capital) that is being invested for your future.

Stocks: The easiest way to think of stocks is to imagine they are tiny pieces of a company. If we related it to a jigsaw puzzle, each puzzle piece would be one stock of the company. All of the puzzle pieces, the stocks, together make up the whole company. You can purchase a single stock or multiple stocks in a company. The place stocks are bought and sold is called the **stock market.**

Bonds: The simplest way to think of bonds is to relate it to an IOU. Have you ever gone to your wallet or your piggy bank and instead of the money you left in it, there was a note from your son or daughter? The note probably said something like "I borrowed your cash, but I'll pay it back on Wednesday when I get paid. Thanks! I love you!" If you had been a savvy investor, you might have even charged some minor interest on that loan. Bonds work the same way.

When a company or a government needs extra capital, they can get it from investors. They issue bonds, which work as IOUs. The bonds pay a yearly interest payment and at the end of a predetermined period, the IOU is cashed in and the loan is repaid. In simplest terms, the bond acts as the paperwork of a loan from an investor, to a company or government. In that paperwork, that IOU from the issuing company or government, are the terms of the loan, the interest to be paid and the due date of repayment.

One last note about bonds – because the risk is typically very low, they are usually incredibly safe investments. However, because the risk is typically very low, they typically do not produce high returns. And finally, because the bond is a loan for a set period of time that pays a set rate of interest, bond returns can be tracked very easily and calculated ahead of time. If you purchase a bond, you will know exactly how much return you will earn in interest every year and when your loan will be repaid.

Mutual Funds: This is the bread and butter of the investment advisor's world. Think of it as the engine that makes most every investment 'go.'

In very basic terms, a mutual fund is an investment account that companies use to pool people's money into for purposes of investing. Once there is enough money (capital), a manager invests that capital into different single or combinations of stocks, bonds, options (we'll talk about 'options' in detail later) and other similar vehicles. Each mutual fund will have a stated goal and will have a stated risk. You can find those goals and risks in the paperwork, called a prospectus, delivered by the company providing the mutual fund. One of the main advantages of a mutual fund is it gives the everyday, normal person access to professionally managed *portfolios*. Those portfolios, which simply mean they are comprised of many different types of stocks, bonds, options, money markets, etc., have a depth of diversification.

There are some positives and some negatives to mutual funds. The positives include: professional management, diversification, they are pretty liquid (meaning you can get a cash equivalent rather easily), the prospectus will list the investment goals and you'll know any inherent risk before you choose to invest. Some negatives with mutual funds include: the rather large fees that many mutual fund companies charge, mutual funds cannot be bought and sold throughout the day for the fluctuating prices (the price is set once per day) and in a negative year, mutual funds can lose a portion or *all of your money*.

Index: An index is a tracking system. Think of it like an imaginary portfolio used to represent any particular market chosen. We could choose 100 different pizza companies, track their stocks and call it the *Pizza Index 100* (sounds tasty). Since stocks are pieces of a company (like pieces in a jigsaw puzzle), and indexes are used to measure how certain stocks are performing, they in turn are measuring how a grouping of companies is performing. For instance, the S&P 500 Index measures the top 500 large cap stocks, representing the leading industries of the US economy. You cannot purchase Index stocks, only the stocks in the company that the index is tracking. In other words, you can't purchase *Pizza Index 100* stocks, but you could purchase stocks from Pizza World, one of the companies inside of the *Pizza Index 100*.

IRA: Also called an Individual Retirement Account, it is a government-sponsored way to save money for retirement. When I say government-sponsored, what I mean is the government allows some special tax rules for IRAs. There are two basic types of IRAs, called the Traditional IRA and the Roth IRA. They both behave very similarly and to keep this simple, we'll talk about some of the basic rules that apply to the IRA. Those rules include maximum amounts that can be contributed into the account each year. They also have penalties for withdrawing gains before the age of 59½ and in the case of the Traditional IRA, there are penalties for not withdrawing money before age 70½. Those mandatory withdrawals are called Required Minimum Distributions (RMDs).

In most instances, the underlying investment vehicle inside an IRA, the engine running this car, is a mutual fund – you get to select the mutual fund or funds you want. Since the mutual fund is the investment vehicle an IRA uses, the IRA has many of the same positives and negatives that a mutual fund has. Positives include: professional management, diversification, liquidity and they also include some government tax advantages. Negatives include: big fees, once a day pricing, possibility of losing all your money and also include limits on how much you can invest per year ($5500 in 2016), when you can access your money, how it is taxed when it is accessed and also when you are required to access your money. There are penalties for getting to *your* money early or not accessing *your* money when the government wants you to.

401(k): This is an employer sponsored retirement plan. Many times, the employer will match the amount (up to a point) that an employee invests in the account. That's FREE MONEY! The 401(k) is a tax-deferred retirement account. The basic premise of a tax-deferred account is that you can invest more of your money now because you aren't being charged taxes before you invest. The trade-off is that your money is taxed when you access it and we really have no idea what tax rate you will be charged when we get to that point. If you wait until retirement age to access your money, you likely won't have the same tax deductions (dependents, house, etc.) that you do as a current worker.

The underlying vehicle that primarily runs most 401(k) plans, the engine that makes this retirement plan 'go,' is a mutual fund. Remember when I said mutual funds were the bread and butter of the investment advisor's world? Are you starting to understand that statement?

Since the engine that primarily runs most 401(k) plans is one or more mutual funds, they have the same positives and negative characteristics as mutual funds in addition to their own, unique characteristics. Positives include professional management, diversification, liquidity, some government tax advantages and FREE MONEY if you happen to be employed by a company that will match your contributions. Negatives include fees, once a day pricing, possibility of losing all your money, when you can access your money, how it is taxed when it is accessed and also when you are required to access your money. Like a Traditional IRA there are penalties for getting to *your* money early or not accessing *your* money when the government wants you to. Another negative is that typically, the plan administrator is the one who decides how or where your money is invested. You want to invest in *Mutual Fund A*? If it's not available in your 401(k), you're out of luck. You'll have to do that on your own.

The First Objection

Our next term to define is **Life Insurance:** If your first inclination was to yell, *"Objection! I object!! Life insurance isn't a retirement vehicle! I heard [insert celebrity name here] on the radio or on the television and they said I shouldn't handle my retirement through life insurance! They said that's a bad plan! They said there are all kinds of fees and expenses! They said 'buy term and invest the rest' and that's what I'm going to do. The famous people said so!"* Let me deal with this right now and then I'll move forward with my definition and description.

Juror Number One, unlike most radio and television personalities out there who claim to be 'experts' on investing and retirement, I actually have the licenses to work in the industry. This is my profession and I do this every day. I help people every day. I live this every day. I've *experienced* how this *Alternate Retirement Plan* works, how it performs, the benefits, the advantages to it. I've experienced them in my own life. Unlike those radio and television personalities, I have these licenses and because of that I am regulated by the government on what I can say, how I can say it, how often and where I can say it. Unlike those radio and television personalities, I am required to attend continuing education classes to stay current on regulations and products. I am required to fulfill a certain number of ethics classes. I am *required* to look out for the best interests of the people I speak with. Those TV and radio personalities aren't regulated, they aren't necessarily looking out for your best interests, they're not required to continue their education on regulations or products. Heck, they might not even care about you, your future or your money (except if you're spending it on their products and their university). They talk for a living. Just keep it in mind.

Right here, the judge would probably say something like – *"I'm going to overrule the objection for now, but I'll leave it up to* Juror Number One *to ultimately decide if they want to follow the industry professional or the TV personality. I caution you* Juror Number One, *to wait until you've finished the book to decide. You agreed to remain unbiased, remember?"*

More Terms and Definitions
(we're almost done with them)

Where were we? Let's go back to the definition of life insurance. **Life insurance**: this is a legal contract between a life insurance company and a policyholder. The policyholder pays money (either monthly, yearly, lump sum, etc.) called a premium, to the life insurance company in return for the promise that the life insurance company will pay a larger lump sum of money to the policyholder's beneficiary in the event the policyholder dies.

There are three basic types of life insurance. Each of those three types of life insurance has many variations and each company that sells life insurance has their own policy quirks. Just so we are on the same page, I'm going to give some very basic descriptions of the three types of life insurance. *Juror Number One*, if you were to come visit me at my office, this is the same way we would start our first conversation about life insurance.

Life insurance, in general, is priced based on a person's gender, their age and their health. There may be some other factors depending on the company (credit score, driving record, etc.), but in general, gender, age and health are the basic measurables. The easiest way I've found to explain the three different types of life insurance is by using an analogy of living spaces.

Rental property...

The first basic type of life insurance is called **Term Life** insurance and to explain Term Life insurance, I use the analogy of renting an apartment. If you were to rent an apartment, you would sign a contract, called a lease, for a certain time period. That lease might be a year, three years or five years. Renting an apartment is relatively inexpensive, especially in comparison to purchasing a house, and there's very little to think about outside of the monthly payment. There's no upkeep or maintenance – you're not required to cut the grass or paint the exterior. At the end of the lease period, you would either have to move out or sign a new lease. It might not be possible to sign a new lease due changes in your credit rating or changes in management or even because of new pricing. If you are still able to sign a new lease, it will probably be more expensive due to economy changes, upkeep expenses, inflation, and the like. More than likely, you will not have the same payment you've grown accustomed to in the original lease.

Renting an apartment is a great solution for many people, especially people on a budget or just starting out in life, but there are other options available. Those other options have added benefits that renting an apartment just doesn't have. For instance, you don't build any equity (cash value) in your apartment, even though you are making a monthly payment and you don't own that apartment or the building you've been paying on. But apartments are cheap and that fills a need in our society.

Term Life insurance works the same way renting an apartment does. You sign a contract for a set time period, called a term, which is typically 10 years, 20 years or 30 years. Renting Term Life insurance is relatively inexpensive, especially in comparison to some of the other life insurance options. There's very little to think about outside of the monthly payment – no upkeep or maintenance. At the end of the term, the insurance either runs out or you'll have to sign a new term contract. This is where things get sticky. Remember when I said, life insurance is based on gender, age and health? If you are able to sign a new term contract, it will be more expensive because you are 10, 20 or 30 years older than when you signed the original contract. After your term expires, your age has changed and possibly your health has too. If you've had certain medical problems like cancer or have suffered a heart attack, among other things, you might not even be eligible to sign a new term. Best case scenario, you're still in good health after 30 years, when your Term Life insurance expires. Now, at 50 or 60 years old, you'll have to prove insurability by undergoing a new health exam and the insurance will be much more expensive than when you were in your twenties or thirties. You have two options at this point – pay for it or go without.

Renting Term Life insurance is a great solution for many people, especially people on a budget or just starting out in life, but there are other options available. Those other options have added benefits that renting Term Life insurance just doesn't have. For instance, you don't build any equity (cash value) in your Term Life insurance, even though you are making a monthly payment. Term life insurance is a great solution for many people, but there are other life insurance solutions available that might be a better fit for where you are in life and the goals you want to accomplish, *Juror Number One*.

Just as an aside, I think it's pretty interesting that you never hear those radio and TV personalities that we mentioned earlier advising people to *"rent an apartment and invest the rest."* Why is that?

For a longer, committed relationship...

The second basic type of life insurance is called **Whole Life** insurance and to explain Whole Life insurance, I use the analogy of purchasing a house. When you purchase a house you get a whole list of benefits that renting an apartment doesn't have. That house is yours. You own it. If you want to paint it in a zebra pattern, you have that ability. If you want to put bars on the windows, go for it. As long as you make the payments, that house belongs to you and the price won't change. The house will build cash value, you can borrow against it (second mortgage) and the house is listed as an asset on any ledger sheet. Here's the thing, typically, buying a house is more expensive than renting an apartment. The house is more expensive and there are other financial considerations to keep in mind – lawn upkeep, trash pick-up, not to mention big ticket expenses like replacing the roof or purchasing homeowners insurance (which caused my monthly payment to fluctuate). When I moved from an apartment to my first house, the difference in monthly payment was a little over $300, but the monthly expense difference was the most staggering thing to me. But it was MY house and it was worth it to me. I was building something – my credit and equity in my house.

Purchasing a house is the best option for some people, even though the cost is considerably higher, in most cases, than renting an apartment. The benefits are worth the cost to them.

Whole Life insurance works in the same fashion. When you purchase Whole Life insurance, you get a whole list of benefits that renting Term Life insurance doesn't have. That life insurance is yours. You own it. It's not going away as long as you pay the premiums and the price never changes! Once you have the insurance, you never have to worry about being insurable. This policy is permanent, meaning it isn't going to run out like renting the Term Insurance, so you'll never have to prove insurability again. Whole Life insurance will build cash value that you can borrow against and Whole Life insurance is listed as an asset on any ledger sheet. But just like buying a house is more expensive than renting an apartment, Whole Life insurance is more expensive than renting Term Insurance. There are other financial considerations to think about as well. Just like when you purchase a home, you have to pay for lawn upkeep, trash pick-up, etc., Whole Life insurance has some administrative costs built in which drives the premium up higher than the relatively maintenance free Term Insurance.

So let's make up some numbers right here. We've talked about renting Term Life insurance and buying Whole Life insurance. Let's plug some completely fictional numbers into our scenarios just for illustration's sake. Let me be clear, we're just making up numbers here for sake of illustration, and if you want to know exact prices for your gender, age and health status, you should see a life insurance professional.

Let's say you, for sake of this illustration, are a young man, in good health and a non-nicotine user. On your 30th birthday, you decide to start a new life insurance policy. To rent 30 years worth of Term Life insurance with a guarantee to pay $250,000 in the case of your death, the premium might run you around $50 a month – for the next 30 years. To purchase the same amount of Whole Life insurance with a guarantee to pay $250,000 in the case of your death, it might cost you somewhere in the neighborhood of $250 a month – for the rest of your life. That's a difference of $200 a month for the next 30 years! If we only took the 30 years that both policies were in force at the same time, it would be a $72,000 difference in premiums paid.

Renting Term Life insurance:
$50 a month
x 12 months a year
x 30 years
 = **$18,000**

Purchasing Whole Life insurance:
$250 a month
x 12 months a year
x 30 years
 = **$90,000**

$90,000 Whole Life insurance premium
- $18,000 Term Life insurance rent
= **$72,000 difference**

Seems like a *'slam dunk'* doesn't it? But then what happens? What happens when that Term Life policy expires? Well, now you're 60 years old and hopefully you're still insurable. If you are, you're probably too old to get another 30-year Term Life policy. The best you can hope to get is a 20-year Term Life policy and to rent that policy for the next 20 years, it will cost you somewhere in the neighborhood of $400 a month – every month for

20 years. Yikes. That will end up being 50 years of rent you've paid into life insurance in your lifetime.

Renting 20 more years of Term Life insurance:
$400 a month
x 12 months a year
x 20 years
 = **$96,000**

Purchasing 20 more years of Whole Life insurance:
$250 a month
x 12 months a year
x 20 years
= **$60,000**

So how much would 50 years of each type of insurance cost us?

Renting Term Life insurance:
$18,000 for the first 30 years
+ $96,000 for the next 20 years
= **$114,000**

Purchasing Whole Life insurance:
$90,000 for the first 30 years
+ $60,000 for the next 20 years
 = **$150,000**

When your 80th birthday rolls around, how much money have you accrued in your Term Life Policy? *Hint: it starts with a 'Z' and rhymes with 'hero.'* Do you get to keep the $114,000 you paid over that 50 year period or do you get to keep even a portion of it? I'm sorry, *Juror Number One*, the answer is no, you don't. You don't get to keep any of it. None. It's gone. Now you are 80 years old, uninsurable and have lost $114,000. Doesn't seem like a sound investment to me, regardless of what those TV personalities say.

On the other hand, if you had purchased Whole Life insurance, you would have paid $150,000 in premiums in those same 50 years. If that was the case, the day after your 80th birthday, you'd simply pay that month's premium of $250 and your coverage would continue. You know what else is pretty cool about that Whole Life policy? You have cash value built up, wrapped in your policy. With the illustration software that my company uses, in this scenario, a very conservative estimate shows you would have in excess of $170,000 worth of cash value in the policy on the 50th anniversary date. That seems like a pretty good investment to me, you've made in excess of $20,000. Remind me again why those TV personalities don't like Whole Life insurance?

Juror Number One, you might be thinking to yourself at this point, *"Is that really the best that life insurance has to offer? I mean, I see the positives to Term Insurance. I really like how affordable it is, but I also know it will expire. I can see the positives to Whole Life insurance, too. I love the fact it never goes away and that it earns me a little money, but it's just more than I want to pay for Life Insurance."*

You're in luck. You might not remember it, but I told you there were **three** basic types of life insurance! Term Life insurance and Whole Life insurance are just the first two versions. There is a third type of life insurance called **Universal Life**.

The Best of Both Worlds...

Universal Life insurance is a type of permanent life insurance, meaning if all conditions are met, the policy will never expire. It's permanent life insurance but it's built on Term principles. Let me repeat that: It's a permanent policy, built on Term principles.

I know what you're thinking. You're probably thinking something like, *"Huh? Do what?!?"* Think of it like this – if Term Life is like renting an apartment and Whole Life is like buying a house, Universal Life Insurance is like a Rent-To-Own contract on a sleek, uptown condo. This condo has all the features you could ever want. This condo is straight off of one of those decorating TV shows, complete with flat screen televisions, a large kitchen with an open floor plan. You name it. This condo has it.

Now, with this rent-to-own contract, you pay a monthly payment. The first half of the payment is used to rent the condo so you can go ahead and live in it now. The second half of the monthly payment is put in a savings account and credited toward the purchase of the condo so the condo will be yours forever. That savings account is even earning you some interest! If you want to add more money into that savings account, go for it. It's just earning you extra money while it sits there. If you decide you don't want the condo or you decide you need some of the money for something else, you can get to it. It's sitting in that savings account waiting on you, holding your 'spot' as condo owner. As long as there is some of the deposit money left in the condo's savings account, it's still counted as *your* condo. This is a contract that will never expire as long as there is a least $1 deposit money left in the savings account and you continue to pay rent.

Universal Life insurance works the same way. Let's use some numbers to explain how this policy works.

Remember in our previous example, with you as a 30 year old man, the premium for the Term Life insurance was $50 a month and the premium for the Whole Life insurance was $250 a month? The premium charged for a Universal Life policy falls somewhere in between Term Life and Whole Life. Just remember, I'm still making all of these numbers up, just for sake of our illustration. For our example, let's imagine the premium charged for $250,000 worth of Universal Life insurance will be $125 a month.

In very general terms, the easiest way to think of it is like this*; of that $125 premium, the first $50 is used by the life company to purchase a month's worth of Term Life Insurance. The company is renting one month's worth of Term Life insurance for you. The remaining $75 goes into an account and is credited to you. Think of it like this, the first $50 rents that sleek, uptown condo for a month (Term Life) while the second $75 goes into an account and is credited towards purchasing the place. The thing to remember is this simple point – that $75 is still your money. You still have access to it. It's yours. Because that money isn't being used to purchase additional life insurance, it is considered cash value inside your policy. But instead of just sitting inside a savings account, the life insurance company actually invests that money for you, where you want it invested, and it grows tax deferred inside that life policy. There is a vast array of available investment options, but ultimately, you get to decide where you want the money invested. *Oh yeah, if you want to invest more than that $75, you can! Any additional money you invest, the more potential you have to earn larger sums of money – because in this account, you earn compounding interest!* You don't know it yet, but those last two sentences are extremely important. We'll get back to it later.

[*While this is the easiest way to think of how Universal Life insurance works and the numbers give a very real picture of the difference in how your money is spent versus invested, life insurance companies divide your premium into a few different places. The premium you pay is still divided between "purchasing insurance" and "investing your money." In our example, the first $50 was used to rent a month's worth of Term Life insurance. That's the portion we are talking about – the first $50, the portion allocated for "purchasing a month's worth of insurance." In reality, the *actual* cost of the monthly insurance is MUCH lower, in the neighborhood of $4 a month, but the life insurance company adds all of their other fees, maintenance costs, administration charges, etc. to that $4, which use up the remaining $46, giving us a total of $50. The other part of the money, in our example that $75, is still yours, to invest where you want within the blanket protection of the life insurance policy.]

"So, what happens as I get older?" you might be thinking. *"You told me earlier, that as I age, Term Life insurance gets more expensive. Isn't that true with this type of life insurance policy, too? Aren't we purchasing Term Life insurance every month? Won't the underlying insurance go up every month, every year?"*

The simple answer is, yes, the underlying insurance cost will go up as you age, but on a yearly basis – not monthly. And when I say there's an increase on a yearly basis, it's going up from $4 a month in the first year to $4.15 a month the second year, up to $4.70 in the next year, up to $5 a month in the third year. In other words, they are very small increases. You can continue to pay the same $125 premium, but now, $51 dollars goes towards the "purchase of insurance" and $74 is "invested" and is credited toward your cash value. The administration charges and fees remain the same for the first 15 or 20 years, depending on the company, and then those charges go down considerably.

I can almost read your mind. *"What happens when I reach the point where the monthly costs are more than the monthly amount that I'm paying? At some point, it's bound to happen. **Gulp!** Do I have to make up the difference?"* The answer is YES and NO.

YES, you have to make up the difference between the actual costs of insurance and the monthly amount you are paying, but NO, it's not going to cost you any more money. You've already made provision for paying those excessive costs. *"I have? How? When?"* You made provision by placing that extra $75 a month for 50 years into your interest earning savings account. Now, when the insurance costs are $400 a month, you simply pay your $125 like normal and that begins to purchase that month's worth of insurance. The remaining $275 needed to purchase the insurance is drawn from your cash value, that money sitting in your savings account. In essence, what we've done is overpay for insurance while we're young and then underpay for insurance when we're older – except that we've been earning compounding interest on that overpayment for all of these years. It's that compounding interest that is so magical. We'll get back to it later in our trial. Look for it in the Evidence section.

One last thing to mention, as I was talking about mutual funds, IRAs, 401(k) plans and other retirement plans, I gave positives and negatives for each. When we get to the Evidence section, I am going to give you all of the positives for Universal Life insurance and when we get to the Circumstantial Evidence section, I'm going to give you all of the negatives. The one negative that mutual funds, IRAs and 401(k) plans have in common is the possibility of losing some or all of your money. All of the retirement plans we've talked about have that in common. They can all lose your life's savings … except the *Alternate Retirement Plan*. In it, you are contractually guaranteed to **never lose any money**. Ready to learn more? Let's find out the history of this plan.

CHAPTER 5
SETTING THE SCENE

Juror Number One, if you were a music junkie, could there possibly be anything more thrilling than seeing your favorite musical artist in concert? Imagine, what would it have been like to see the Beatles in Shae Stadium if you had been their biggest fan in 1965? You probably knew of their history, Germany and the Cavern Club up to the Ed Sullivan Show. You could sing all the words to all their songs. You probably had adopted their way of dress and their mannerisms. You might have even gotten that trademark *mop top* Beatles haircut. It's true there were a lot of people that didn't care for the Beatles. They didn't follow them at all, didn't know their history. They didn't know any of the words to the songs, didn't care about their style or their hair. It would have been hard to relate to that person how *dreamy* Paul was or how much better of a drummer Ringo was compared to Pete Best, if they didn't even know who the members of the band were!

The way that fan felt about the Beatles is the same way I feel about the *Alternate Retirement Plan*. I'm a fan. Let's learn the history of the *Alternate Retirement Plan* band so we can sing all of the words to the song together.

To set the stage, let's read a paragraph from Gregory Bresinger's article on Investopedia.com entitled *The Great Inflation of the 1970's*.

> "It's the 1970s, and the stock market is a mess. It loses 40% in an 18-month period, and for close to a decade few people want anything to do with stocks. Economic growth is weak, which results in rising unemployment that eventually reaches double-digits. The easy-money policies of the American central bank, which were designed to generate full employment, by the early 1970s, also caused high inflation. The central bank, under different leadership, would later reverse its policies, **raising interest rates to some 20%**, a number once considered usurious. For interest-sensitive industries, such as housing and cars, **rising interest rates** cause a calamity. With **interest rates skyrocketing,** many people are priced out of new cars and homes. This is the gruesome story of the great

inflation of the 1970s, which began in late 1972 and didn't end until the early 1980s."[1] (Added emphasis is mine – you'll see why momentarily.)

As you can see, by the early 1980's the American economy was hurting. Unemployment was up, inflation was up, and interest rates were up – way up. The prime interest rate peaked on December 19, 1980, when it hit 21.5%. It has never been that high since. To put it in perspective at the time I'm writing this book in 2016, the prime interest rate is 3.5% and has been under 5% since April of 2008.

Insurance companies wanted a way for their clients to maximize their retirement funds and they decided they had the perfect solution. You guessed it, their perfect solution worked by tapping into the interest rate market inside of a Traditional Universal Life policy. This was actually a stroke of genius because of how interest rates were performing at the time – there was great big money to be made!

Traditional Universal Life

Insurance agents started generating paperwork to show their clients how much money could be made in a Traditional Universal Life policy. These forms, which are technically named *Hypothetical Illustrations* and which are still used today, are meant to show a client how the investment portion of their premium paid **might** perform (in addition to other things). That's the key word **MIGHT**, how their investment **might** perform. Insurance agents and the companies they represented had no way of knowing what interest rates would do. For all they knew, the interest rates could keep going up or level off never to return to single digits again. So when they calculated their illustrations, they showed their clients great looking hypothetical returns based on incredibly high interest rates that never dipped to their previous levels. It looked like an untapped gold mine! And, it would have been if interest rates had stayed in the double digits. Which leads us back to what my cousin Joel always says, "If something looks too good to be true, it *probably* is."

The Prime interest rate peaked in December of 1980 and began an almost steady decline that has lasted, with very few exceptions, until today in 2016. It's only been in the double digits one time since May of 1985 and that was only for a very brief period of time. The way these Traditional Universal Life policies had been built, was on the premise that the investment portion of the premium would generate a generous supply of money so the insurance companies didn't collect as much premium as was needed to keep the policies in force. Then, when the interest rates started falling, the money that had been invested in the Life Policy wasn't enough to sustain the policy. Incredible amounts of Traditional Universal Life policies were underfunded and were surrendered due to lack of funds.

If we relate it to our earlier, "rent-to-own" illustration and that sleek, uptown condo, it would be like the landlord coming to you one day, *Juror Number One*, and telling you that when she set up the contract and you agreed to pay the rent, she realized she wasn't charging you enough rent. Since she wasn't charging you the correct amount, your landlord decided to start getting the difference from your savings account. That savings account was just barely earning you any interest, but she didn't know that. Your landlord was certain the interest from the account would produce plenty of money for you to keep your savings *and* pay the rent. But she was wrong! Now that your funds are depleted, you are being forced to move out. Your contract for that condo has been surrendered through no fault of your own.

Wouldn't you be upset with your landlord if she told you that you didn't have any money in your savings account because *she* hadn't been charging you enough rent? Wouldn't you be mad if she then told you that you had to move out and you realized you didn't have any place to go? That's what happened with a lot of Traditional Universal Life policyholders in the 1980s. They were unintentionally (I believe) misled, by those insurance agents and companies based on short-term interest rate behavior. It was an error in judgment by the life companies and the also the policyholders that led to thousands of policies across the country being surrendered.

As you can imagine, there were scores of unhappy people. They were unhappy with investing in general, unhappy with insurance agents, unhappy with insurance companies and they were especially unhappy with the Traditional Universal Life policy.

Where do we go from here?

So, what happened next? The timeframe was the late 80's into the 1990's. Did everybody just start digging holes and burying their savings in the back yard? Well, I'm sure there was some of that, but the stock market was BOOMING. People were making money hand over fist. Hollywood was making movies about Wall Street and the money flowing out. The economic processes in place at the time were working. The economy was strong and there was money to be made.

People were already unhappy with the interest rate method being used inside of the Traditional Life policies, but when they saw the soaring gains being made in the stock market, the public began to demand a "stock market" version of the Universal Life policy. At that same time, insurance companies were realizing that the interest rate method inside of the Traditional Universal Life policy wasn't working the way they had intended, and were already wondering if they could use a different method instead. Out of the failure of the Traditional Universal life policy to do what the industry *thought* it should do and the strong public demand, life companies began investigating the idea of tying the investment portion inside a Universal Life policy, not to interest rates, but directly to the stock market. That's the next iteration of Universal Life policies we're going to briefly look at.

Before we completely move to the next type of Universal Life policy that came to the market place, I should say that even though there were some failures on the part of the participants (life company reps and policyholders) with the Traditional Universal Life, the policy itself did what it was *supposed* to do. It earned money, very small but safe amounts, inside of a life insurance policy. The problem with the policy was the fact that life agents didn't understand how and why it worked. Remember, people were making money with the Traditional Universal Life, just not much. It is still a policy that is issued today, with decent (not stellar) results. People are a little bit happier with it today and their expectations are a little more realistic because the insurance agents run the hypothetical illustrations in a much more realistic manner.

Variable Universal Life

So we move to the next policy that came to the Universal Life insurance market. It was wearing a red cape and had a giant "V" on its chest. The **Variable Universal Life** policy, typically called a **VUL**, came to the marketplace to save all of those potential investors from the poor returns they were getting on their "investment portion" causing their Traditional Universal Life policies to cancel. The insurance companies decided that allowing the customers to invest directly in the stock market would allow them access to the untapped world of those stock market gains. It would also pass the responsibility of any gains or losses away from interest rates and directly to the customer.

To make this Variable Universal Life policy possible, it was brought to the market place with higher fees, charges and administrative costs than the Traditional Universal Life policy. Basically, it cost the life insurance companies more money to use the stock market approach than using the interest rate approach, and they passed those costs on to the customer. In everyone's eyes (the customer and the life companies alike), those costs wouldn't play a big role, because of how much potential there was to make money in the stock market.

In very simple terms, the way the VUL policy works is very similar to the way the Traditional

Universal Life policy works: A portion of the monthly premium is used to purchase a month's worth of term insurance (plus those higher fees, charges and administration costs) and a portion is used to invest in the stock market. Because of the higher fees, charges and administration costs, more money is charged in the "insurance" portion and less is actually invested. In our example, let's pretend the split has swapped and now, $75 is being charged for rent and only $50 is being invested. The underlying fund (the stock market portion) is typically mutual funds and as such, the VUL has the additional positives and negatives that come with mutual funds.

Time Marches On…

It was the late 80's and moving into the 90's. Times were good! The economy was still booming and people were making all sorts of money. Now, in a rising economy the Variable Universal Life policy is unequaled. The sky is the limit! As long as the economy is performing and as long as stock prices are up, the VUL policy really is second to none because you are partaking in all of the growth of the underlying mutual fund! You don't have to share any of that growth with the insurance company (or anyone else for that matter). You get it all! People were falling over themselves to purchase this type of life insurance policy (not literally, but I'm just trying to prove a point here). There was money to be made!

All of this sounds pretty good, doesn't it? Almost sounds too good to be true, doesn't it? What does my cousin Joel always say? "If something looks too good to be true, it *probably* is." People should probably listen to my cousin Joel a *little* more.

People, and that includes both the life insurance companies and the policyholders, didn't learn from the interest rate approach to Universal Life. If they had, they would have learned that just because something goes up, like those interest rates, there is also the possibility it will go down. If the people in the late 80's and into the 90's had learned that lesson, they might have prevented the loss of their money. (That's called foreshadowing!)

The beauty of the Variable Universal Life policy is that there isn't a cap on how much money you can earn inside of the policy. If your underlying stock earns 38% in a year, you get 38% growth added to your cash value in your VUL. If your underlying stock earns 50% in a year, you get 50% growth added to your cash value! Here's the problem though, if your underlying stock loses money in a year – you get all of that loss subtracted from your cash value. So, if your underlying stock loses 38% or 50% in a year, your cash value will also lose the equivalent value. Remember, you get all of the negatives associated with the underlying fund in your policy. One of the negatives with mutual funds is that you can lose all of your money. Added to the negative of a mutual fund being able to lose all your money is the fact that you are still being charged higher fees and administration costs. It's a *'double whammy!'* The money is being lost in the falling market and the remainder is being eaten by high costs. I'm guessing you can see where this is going…

Think back. It's the 90's. Turning on your huge, boxy computer and connecting to the internet lead to fifteen minutes of modem-screeching that sounded like two rival gangs of cats in a turf war. If you were lucky, you got to hear your three favorite words, *"You've got mail!"* And as long as nobody called you and broke the internet connection, you would get to read that one email… from a Nigerian prince who wanted to give you millions of dollars! The age of the internet had been born!

Beginning in about 1995, companies began investing heavily in anything that had *".com"* attached to its name. It didn't matter if that DotCom produced a product or rendered a service, if it had a *".com"* at the end of its name, it would have no problem finding financing. Money was pouring in. The stock market was soaring and it was inundated with DotComs. VUL policyholders saw tremendous increase in their cash value during this time because they were invested in the stock market.

POP!

Then, in March of 2000, the stock market peaked at over *double* the March 1999 market level. The price was so high, that a couple of the movers-and-shakers in the tech world (Dell and Cisco) decided to sell a large portion of their stocks to capitalize on all of that money to be made. But it freaked people out and suddenly, there was a panic. People scrambled to sell their stocks before there wasn't any money left to be made. The stock market began to tumble. By 2001, trillions of dollars had been lost and a majority of those DotCom companies had folded. The stock market and US economy were devastated.

What happened to people who owned Variable Universal Life policies when the DotCom bubble burst? Just like every other investor, they lost money. BIG money. As was the case with people who owned Traditional Universal Life policies a decade earlier, owners of VUL policies failed to realize that what goes up, can also come down and they lost vast amounts of money when the stock market crashed in 2000. When there was no longer any cash value in the VUL policy, the policies were terminated (just like the Traditional Universal Life policy owners had done a decade earlier).

What happened then?

There were several years of negative returns, but eventually, the market somewhat rebounded and began to produce positive results again. Then, the unfathomable happened in 2008. The housing market crashed. The closest thing I can relate this to is the sinking of the *Titanic*.

The *RMS Titanic* was the world's largest, the strongest, the most perfect ship ever built up to that point in time. It was set to revolutionize intercontinental travel. It was hailed as unsinkable. Nobody saw sinking as an even remote possibility or they would have had many more lifeboats aboard. We've all heard the stories and seen the movies. In April of 1912, the *Titanic* collided with an iceberg and within a few hours, sank.

In the same way, people saw that the housing market had always been stable. Always. I'm not going to get into the depths of *how* it all happened but that 'stability' was nothing more than a house of cards built on the sand of a peaceful looking beach. Little did anyone know, there was a tidal wave bearing down on that shoreline… an iceberg to the housing market's *Titanic*.

The housing market came crashing down. The stock market imploded. The US economy fell and saw the worst recession since The Great Depression began in 1929. The world economy was weakened. People lost homes. People lost their pensions and retirement funds.

VUL policyholders were *again* devastated, meaning

more Variable Universal Life policies were surrendered due to lack of funds. Many VUL account holders began to think, that their money would have been safer in a savings account at the bank. They might not earn much, but at least it's never going away and at least they'll never lose any of it! They had a bad VUL taste in their mouth.

In fairness, the Variable Universal Life policy is genuinely a spectacular product, any time the market isn't suffering a negative return, and is still sold by life companies today. It provides more upside growth potential than any life product sold, but as we've seen, it also has a (huge!) downside – just like mutual funds, IRAs, 401(k) plans etc. have. When the housing market crashed, the spectacular VUL fell flat on its face and left many people without life policies and all of that cash value that was once in them.

So, where does that leave us? Really, it leaves us with a bunch of angry people, a decent life policy with some considerable flaws and a horrible reputation and the people in the Universal Life industry with considerable mud on their faces.

Don't worry. The fix is in(dex).

---

[1]*The Great Inflation of the 1970's.* Gregory Bresinger
http://www.investopedia.com/articles/economics/09/1970s-great-inflation.asp#ixzz4Dwcfkd1m

CHAPTER 6
THE FIX IS IN(DEX)

Juror Number One, I asked you a question earlier in this case. I want to keep our ultimate focus on those points so let me remind you of it right here and then we'll continue.

I asked you the question: What would you think if I told you that I was going to give you an investment vehicle that would:

1. Capture market gains whenever they occur;
2. NEVER participate in market losses;
3. Lock in the money you earn each year, so you could never lose it;
4. Allow you to access your money, even your gains, tax free;
5. Allow you to access your money for any reason, at any time and at any age without penalty;

6. Allow you to keep your money invested for as long as you like without penalty;

7. Be protected if you're sued or involved in a lawsuit (depending on the laws of your state);

8. Provide a large, income-tax free, payment to the person of your choosing if you died prematurely;

9. Allow a portion to be accelerated for purposes of chronic illness, acting in the stead of long-term care (without charge until activated)?

The Next Step

With the collapse of the stock market twice in one decade, and with the vast fortunes that were lost, people started thinking that having their money invested in the stock market wasn't as great as they originally thought it was. They realized, there's no safety, no protection of their assets inside the investment portion of the policy. The life insurance companies also realized that having their client's money invested in the stock market wasn't the *best* product they could provide for their customers either. So they went back to the drawing board and took their time to come up with another, better option.

The life insurance companies did their homework. They did research. They plotted and they planned.

They said to themselves, "What are the great things about Universal Life insurance and what are the problems with Universal Life insurance?" They made a list and did their best to keep the good stuff while eliminating the bad stuff. (If only I could do that to my diet!)

The life insurance companies decided to **keep** these existing features:

1. The Life insurance portion. The contractual guarantee that the life company will pay a death benefit to a beneficiary if premiums are paid and there is cash value in the policy;
2. The "investment portion" so money could grow tax-deferred inside the life insurance policy;
3. Some of the administration costs and fees (somebody has to pay it);

Then the life company wondered if they could **eliminate** these negative features in the Universal Life policies:

1. The ability for the customer to lose money;
2. Negative market risk.

Then, the life insurance companies asked these questions about **adding** some new features to the Universal Life policies, like:

1. Could they guarantee the customer would never lose any of their investment capital?

2. Could they find a way for the customer to take advantage of the stock market when it was doing well?

3. Could they find a way to guarantee the customer would never lose any of the money their investment earned? Could the customer "lock-in" their gains?

4. Could they find a way to provide some long-term care insurance built into the policy in the event it was needed (but not charge the customer, just in case it wasn't needed)?

Through hard work, serious math calculations, some common sense and the knowledge of numerous insurance and investing geniuses, the life companies realized they could accomplish all of those things wrapped in a new type of Universal Life policy. They could keep the good things, the things that worked in a Universal Life policy. They could eliminate many negative things about the existing Universal Life policies. And then, they realized they could supply some new, positive attributes to the policy. The fix was in. When the life insurance companies brought this product to the marketplace, they inadvertently created something else. They created the *Alternate Retirement Plan* ... and they didn't even know it!

Index Universal Life

Are you still with me *Juror Number One*? Is your head spinning?

Let me break it down and give you the basics. The **Index Universal Life** policy, also called an **IUL** policy, works in very similar ways that its cousins, the Traditional Universal Life and Variable Universal Life policies did. There is a portion used to purchase a month's worth of insurance and another portion set aside as the "investment" portion. The main difference in the Index Universal life is in how the "investment" portion is handled. The IUL partakes in the market gains but **does not** participate in market losses – ever. There is a limit, called a cap, on how much of the gains a policy can keep, but there is a floor, which protects from any losses. That means, you can earn up to the cap when the market is doing well and never lose any of your investment capital if the market crashes.

I know what you're probably thinking right about now, *Juror Number One, "What about your cousin Joel? Doesn't he always say, 'If it sounds too good to be true, it probably is'? Honestly, this sounds **way too good to be true**!"*

I promise, I'm not a mind-reader, it's just the exact same thing I thought when I was first introduced to this policy. Let's examine this policy a little more closely and find out if my cousin Joel is right or if this is the exception to his rule.

How it works...

We are about to get into some very technical stuff.

I'll keep it short and as easy to understand as possible. Regardless of whether you understand this portion, just realize it is built on solid mathematical calculations and contractually guaranteed to perform in this manner.

Remember back in Chapter Three we gave a bunch of definitions? Here's the time you might want to go back and get a quick refresher. Go back and look at the section on **BONDS.** If you'll think back, *Juror Number One,* I told you that because the bond is a loan for a set period of time that pays a set rate of interest, bond returns can be tracked very easily and calculated ahead of time. If you purchase a bond, you will know exactly how much return you will earn every year in interest and when your loan will be repaid. The ability of the insurance company to guarantee your floor of zero (guaranteeing you will never lose any money), is based on bonds.

For this section, let's only consider the investment portion of the premium you pay. The insurance company takes the money you invest, and places the majority of it in bonds (let's imagine it's 95%). The insurance company knows exactly how much the bond will pay in interest and when it will be paid, so they know *exactly* when the portion invested in bonds will equal the total amount invested. It might be easier to understand using actual, simplified figures. Imagine you invest $100. The insurance company invests $95 of that money in bonds. The bonds are safe and predictable. Within a year, that $95 will have grown back to $100. So that takes care of the floor, our downside protection. So, even if the market drops, you won't lose your $100!

But how do we also get to participate in the gains the market may take? And what happens to that other $5?

In the financial world, there's a term called an "Option." Options are extremely complex in nature, but I will try and simplify them here. Realize this is just one small facet of Options and they are incredibly versatile in nature.

Think of it like this – you go to Vegas, end up at the roulette table and want to place a bet. There are a lot of different ways you can place your bet – complex ways, betting on certain numbers or certain colors or even certain combinations. I want to focus on the easiest way you can bet – either RED or BLACK. All you have to do is set your chips down on that color square, and if the little ball lands on your color, you win.

The Options that I want to focus on, in a weird way, work in the same manner. They are called Put Options and Call Options (Puts and Calls). These are our RED and BLACK color squares.

Puts and Calls deal exclusively with the *direction* of a given index. That index is either going to go up or it is going to go down – one way or the other. Puts, our RED color, make money when the index goes down. Calls, our BLACK color, make money when the index goes up.

In essence, the insurance company takes the remaining portion of the investment (the remaining 5%) and sets it down on the BLACK color, the Call Option. If the index goes up, the Call Option pays. If the Call Option pays, we make money in our investment portion of our Index Universal Life policy. If the index goes down (the RED color), the insurance company loses the "bet" but our bond funds secure our floor and even though the rest of the economy may tank, we don't lose a penny.

Now, don't worry. The insurance company isn't gambling with your money, but in a nutshell, *Juror Number One*, in the easiest way I know to explain Options in this *Court of Law*, that's how the process works. In reality, it's a bit more complicated, with a few more moving parts, but at its core, that's how the Index Universal Life policy's investment portion operates.

And now that we've seen how it works, what does that mean? How is that useful? What does any of this have to do with the *Alternate Retirement Plan*? *Juror Number One*, prepare to be amazed…

CHAPTER 7
THE EVIDENCE (PART 1)

In a court of law, I would imagine – or at least on TV, the lawyers introduce many pieces of evidence to the jury. Some things seem unrelated and some are obviously tied to the case, but at the end of the session, the lawyer brings them all together and reveals how all the pieces fit together. That's my intent today with the *Alternate Retirement Plan.*

So far, *Juror Number One*, in this case, we've discussed different retirement vehicles, 401(k), IRAs, mutual funds, stocks, bonds, the stock market and we've talked about life insurance and how the different policies work. We've paid special attention to the history and development of the different Universal Life policies and we've looked in depth at how specifically the Index Universal Life Policy works.

But, let's quit talking about the technical aspects of Index Universal Life insurance and start laying out the case for why The Index Universal Life Policy is the most incredible, fantastic, money-making, money-retaining, retirement plan available today. That's right, the Index Universal Life Policy **IS** the *Alternate Retirement Plan*! The *Alternate Retirement Plan* is life insurance you don't have to die to use!

It is a life policy first and foremost and as such it has some things in common with life policies in general, but it also has some wonderful additional properties, which make it a fantastic retirement tool and *Alternate Retirement Plan.* It truly is an *alternate* to the retirement plans we are more familiar with. So let me lay out for you the evidence of why I believe this policy works so much better than all of the other retirement tools we have at our disposal today.

A Hope for Theirs...

My first two pieces of evidence are purely life insurance features – the first is the death benefit. With what other type of retirement vehicle can you invest a minimal amount of money and if you leave this world, just moments after investing, your beneficiary is entitled to a large, income tax-free, lump of money? Granted, the death benefit doesn't do anything towards *your* retirement, but it can leave your beneficiary with a hope for theirs.

Evidence #1 – the death benefit

The second piece of evidence is pretty cut and dried. Because the life insurance is a contract between an insurance company and an insured to pay a death benefit to a specific beneficiary, the death benefit avoids probate. Not sure what probate is? It's one of the worst things to have to go through when a loved one dies. Typically, probate involves paperwork and court appearances by lawyers to identify and inventory the deceased person's possessions, to pay debts and taxes, and then distributing the remaining property according to state law. The lawyers and court fees are paid from estate property, which would otherwise go to the people who inherit the deceased person's property. So instead of inheriting your loved ones possessions, they are used to pay taxes.

The Index Universal Life Policy avoids probate altogether because of the contract status life insurance holds. The *Alternate Retirement Plan* just keeps getting better and better.

Evidence #2 – avoids probate

As we've talked about, tied to this life insurance policy is an investment portion. For the remainder of this chapter, unless otherwise noted, we will only be discussing this portion, the investment portion, of the life policy.

Cash and the Benefits of having it…

My next few pieces of evidence are all tied to the cash value of the account. The third piece of evidence is the fact that this retirement vehicle gives us the ability to accumulate cash. It wouldn't do us any good to be able to put extra money into this policy and then have to withdraw it immediately, would it? No, in this vehicle, we are able add additional money and to leave the money in the account. That additional money, the money you have invested and any gains, gets added to your death benefit. If you were to die, your beneficiary would receive the death benefit *as well as* everything you have invested and earned. One other benefit is that you can always make a tax-free withdrawal of the amount you've paid into the investment – just like a Roth IRA.

Evidence #3 – cash accumulation

This leads me to evidence number four, upside growth potential. *Juror Number One*, what good does it do to add money into an investment if it doesn't have any potential for growth? In this retirement vehicle, there is room to grow. Sure, there is a cap on how much growth you can keep, but there is *plenty* of room to grow! The insurance companies cap the growth on these policies somewhere in the line of 12% to 14%, depending on the company. 12% growth is still HUGE! It is a small price to pay to give up a small amount of growth when considering the alternatives – like losing your life savings – but I'm getting ahead of myself. Do you understand what I mean when I say there is a cap on the growth, *Juror Number One*?

It works like this: let's pretend our account has a 12% cap. If the index earns 9% interest in a year, your account earns 9%. If the index earns 3% in a year, your account earns 3%. If the index earns 17%, you only earn 12%, your cap. The insurance company absorbs the additional 5% the index made. (But that means you still made 12% in your retirement account!!)

Evidence #4 – room to grow

What good would it do us if we had the ability to accumulate and grow our cash but then we had to pay taxes on it every year? What's that you say, *Juror Number One*? That's the way bank CD's work? And mutual funds? You're a little more savvy than I gave you credit for! Good thing we have the *Alternate Retirement Plan!* Evidence number four is tax-deferred growth inside the policy. The money is working, tied to an index, and as it grows, so does your cash value in your account. It's not taxed until you make a withdrawal, so as long as you leave it alone, you don't have to pay taxes on the growth. That leaves more money in the account to earn more interest and make you more money.

Evidence #5 – tax-deferred growth

Everybody should use protection…

I was recently watching a movie that was set in medieval England. The English were at war with France (surprise, surprise). The two armies had gathered on the battlefield and as one of the kings was trying to rally his troops to victory, the enemy launched a volley of arrows – thousands and thousands of them. The sky became black as the arrows arched through the sky. *"Protect the King! Protect the King!"* someone shouted and without hesitation a dozen foot soldiers with shields encircled the king, completely covering him. It looked like a medieval turtle as the arrows clanged and bounced off the protective covering.

How would you like for your investment to be protected, like that king was, against the arrows of market losses? Any time the market took a negative turn, it just bounced right off of your account, never affecting it? Well, evidence number five is protection against market losses. We have seen how the policy works using bonds as a hedge of protection against market losses, but let's take a closer look at what that actually means.

Juror Number One, I would like to enter into the record, *Evidence Exhibit A*, the S&P 500 returns.

The following chart is the actual returns of the S&P 500 from 1995 until 2015. In that 20-year period, 14 years made positive gains, 1 year was level and we only experienced 5 negative years.

How much money would be in an account that was tied to the index that benefitted from all of the gains, but also suffered all of the losses? Let's imagine we had invested $1000 on 12/30/1995. How much money would be in our account today?

I give you *Evidence Exhibit A:*

Begin – End date	Index Change	$1,000
12/31/95 – 12/31/96	22.87%	$1228.70
12/31/96 – 12/31/97	31.01%	$1609.72
12/31/97 – 12/31/98	26.67%	$2039.03
12/31/98 – 12/31/99	19.53%	$2437.25
12/31/99 – 12/31/00	-10.14% (DotCom bubble)	$2190.11
12/31/00 – 12/31/01	-12.06%	$1925.98
12/31/01 – 12/31/02	-23.37%	$1475.88
12/31/02 – 12/31/03	26.38%	$1865.22
12/31/03 – 12/31/04	8.99%	$2032.90
12/31/04 – 12/31/05	3.00%	$2093.89
12/31/05 – 12/31/06	13.62%	$2379.08
12/31/06 – 12/31/07	4.24%	$2479.95
12/31/07 – 12/31/08	-38.49% (Housing bubble)	$1525.42

12/31/08 – 12/31/09	23.45%	$1883.13
12/31/09 – 12/31/10	12.78%	$2123.79
12/31/10 – 12/31/11	0.00%	$2123.79
12/31/11 – 12/31/12	11.52%	$2368.45
12/31/12 – 12/31/13	29.60%	$3069.51
12/31/13 – 12/31/14	11.39%	$3419.13
12/31/14 – 12/31/15	-0.73%	$3169.53

As you can see from *Evidence Exhibit A*, at the end of the 20-year period, our initial investment of $1000 had grown to over $3000! Even experiencing those 5 years of loss, we still made money! Our average growth for those 20 years was **over 8%**!

Each year's return added together and divided by 20 years gives us our average yearly return %:

160.26 total return
÷ 20 years
= **8.013% average return**

Now, *Juror Number One*, I would like to enter into the record, *Evidence Exhibit B*, the S&P 500 returns with a cap and a floor.

Let's take those same figures, from *Exhibit A*, and imagine them inside an Index Universal Life Policy. In that investment, there is a 12% cap and a 0%

floor. Remember, these are the actual returns from the S&P 500 over the last 20-year period. What would it have looked like if we had $1000 in the investment portion of an IUL on December 30, 1995?

I give you *Evidence Exhibit B:*

Begin – End date	Index Change	Cap/Floor	$1000
12/31/95 – 12/31/96	22.87%	12.00%	$1120.00
12/31/96 – 12/31/97	31.01%	12.00%	$1254.40
12/31/97 – 12/31/98	26.67%	12.00%	$1404.93
12/31/98 – 12/31/99	19.53%	12.00%	$1573.52
12/31/99 – 12/31/00	-10.14%	0.00%	$1573.52
12/31/00 – 12/31/01	-12.06%	0.00%	$1573.52
12/31/01 – 12/31/02	-23.37%	0.00%	$1573.52
12/31/02 – 12/31/03	26.38%	12.00%	$1762.34
12/31/03 – 12/31/04	8.99%	8.99%	$1920.77
12/31/04 – 12/31/05	3.00%	3.00%	$1978.39
12/31/05 – 12/31/06	13.62%	12.00%	$2215.80
12/31/06 – 12/31/07	4.24%	4.24%	$2309.74
12/31/07 – 12/31/08	-38.49%	0.00%	$2309.74
12/31/08 – 12/31/09	23.45%	12.00%	$2586.91

12/31/09 – 12/31/10	12.78%	12.00%	$2897.34
12/31/10 – 12/31/11	0.00%	0.00%	$2897.34
12/31/11 – 12/31/12	11.52%	11.52%	$3231.11
12/31/12 – 12/31/13	29.60%	12.00%	$3618.84
12/31/13 – 12/31/14	11.39%	11.39%	$4031.03
12/31/14 – 12/31/15	-0.73%	0.00%	$4031.03

Can you see why the turtle shield of protection against the arrows of market loss is so important? Even with having a cap of 12%, because we were protected against 5 years of market losses, just 5 years out of a 20-year span, we made almost $1000 more money in our investment. And, did I mention, these are actual returns from the S&P 500? *Juror Number One*, are you beginning to see how incredible this investment vehicle really is?

Evidence #6 – protection against market losses

I'd like to also point out our average return percentage in the IUL. It looks like this:
Each year's return added together and divided by 20 years gives us our average yearly return %:

147.14 total return
÷ 20 years
= **7.357% average return**

Interesting that the average return in *Exhibit B* (7.357%) is less than in *Exhibit A* (8.013%), yet we've made more money (that's called foreshadowing).

True but deceptive…

Recently, my sister was given two, cute, little fur-ball kittens. I was driving home from work when she called and told me about them and invited me and my wife, Lauren, to come "meet" them. I decided I would just call my wife and tell her to change out of her work clothes and be ready to jump in the car in 10 minutes when I got home. She probed and probed about where we were going and why. I told Lauren that my sister had just gotten something and we were going to check it out. Lauren couldn't leave it alone and started guessing:

"Is it a puppy?" No. I'm not telling what it is.

"Is it new furniture?" No. I'm not telling what it is.

"Is it a new car?" No. I'm not telling what it is.

"Is it a kitten?" Umm, no. I'm not telling you what it is. Quit asking!

Can you see what I did there? Technically, it wasn't *A* kitten, it was *two* kittens. So, technically, what I said was true, but it was certainly deceptive. True but deceptive. I simply didn't want to ruin the surprise. I ended up telling her the truth before we ever left the house – my integrity (and her curiosity) wouldn't let me keep it from her.

Investment companies have a surprise built in for you and they've been telling you some things that are completely true, but certainly deceptive as well. Curious?

If you look in any mutual fund literature, even the advertisements, you'll find most financial companies give their average returns over given periods of time – typically, it's something like 1 year, 5 year, 10 year and lifetime. Seeing those averages, which are completely true, gives the impression that you'll see that type of growth from your investment. The averages are true, but that implied growth is deceptive.

I'd like to enter *Evidence Exhibit C*, a simple math formula: If we invest $1000 in a mutual fund and in the first year it loses 50%, the second year it gains 50% and the third year it gains 9%, the *average* for those three years is a 3% gain.

-50% + 50% + 9% = 9%
$\underline{\div 3 \text{ years}}$
= **positive 3%** *average* **for the three years**.

The (deceptive) implication would be that we would make 3% on our $1000 ($30) for a total $1030 at the end of those three years.

In actuality, that is *not* what our $1000 looks like at

the end of three years. $817.50 is what you would have left. In case you're not really good at math, that's less money than you started with even though you *averaged* a **positive 3%.**

Here's the math: The first year you started with $1000 and *lost* 50%. That dropped your $1000 down to $500. The second year, you *earned* 50% ($250), which raised your $500 up to $750. The third year, you *earned* 9% ($67.50) on your $750 taking the grand total up to $817.50. So, while you had a positive *average* of 3%, you are actually in the hole almost 20%. See, the averages are pretty meaningless if you have to factor in a negative number. There is always the possibility of negative numbers in investment vehicles that can lose money. The average is true, but the reality is deceptive. Don't worry, though. I've got great news!

With the *Alternate Retirement Plan*, the Index Universal Life policy, there are NO negative numbers to work into our calculations. That means that the averages and the actual returns will always be accurate. Evidence number six is accurate return figures because we don't have to average in negative numbers.

Enter into record, *Evidence Exhibit D:* Let's pretend now that we are investing $1000 in an IUL policy. We'll use the same formula as before. The index drops 50% the first year, gains 50% the second year, and in the third year it gains 9%. What does that look like to our investment and how much money have we made or lost?

Well, in the first year, we have a floor of ZERO, so we don't lose any money. The second year, we have a cap of 12% and in the third year we earn all 9% the index earns.

0% + 12% + 9% = 21%

÷ 3 years

 = **positive 7% average return for the three years.**

What does our initial $1000 investment look like? In the first year, we don't lose any money, so we stay right at $1000. The second year, even though the index went up 50% we were capped at 12%, so our $1000 investment has now grown to $1120. The third year, our $1120 made another 9%, which raised our total up to $1330. The last time I checked, $1330 was more money than $817.50.

Here's another scenario, *Evidence Exhibit E*: We invest $1000. The index goes down 50% the first year, down another 50% the second year and then finally grows 9% the third year. In our Index Universal Life policy, because we have a floor of 0, we have averaged 3% growth. Here's the math:

0% + 0% + 9% = 9%

÷ 3 years

 = **3% positive average**

(exactly like in *Evidence Exhibit C*).

However, since we didn't have to factor in a negative number, how much money do we have left in our investment? We have a positive *average* of 3%, but what about our *actual* return. Will it be a 20% loss like *Evidence Exhibit C*? Here's what it looks like: $1000 initial investment doesn't lose a penny in year one or two and then grows 9%, up to $1090 in year number three. Positive *average* growth AND positive *actual* growth!

Evidence #7 – accurate return figures

The secret recipe...

When I was dating the woman of my dreams, Lauren, (who would later become my wife) we went on a tour in Atlanta. She's not big into museums... or tours... or reading each and every sign... like I am. However, on this tour we had a very funny tour guide and he told us a story that was so engaging, he kept my wife's attention, and mine, the entire time.

Our tour guide was much funnier than I am, but the story went something like this. A man invented what has become a very famous brand of soft drink. It tasted so good, was so refreshing and it was so extremely addictive (it contained cocaine), that everybody wanted to know the secret recipe. What were the secret ingredients? He never wrote it down. Over the years, he changed and modified the recipe (removing the cocaine) until he eventually sold the company. At that point, he divulged the ingredients to the new owners who committed the recipe to memory. In 1919, the recipe was used as collateral for a loan and the bank made the owners put the recipe in writing. They locked it in a vault inside a bank for safekeeping. See, the secret ingredients are what made the soft drink "work" and without it, it just wouldn't "taste right."

The *Alternate Retirement Plan*, the IUL, has a secret ingredient of its own. This secret ingredient (that's not so secret) is what makes this retirement plan "taste right." Evidence number eight and the secret ingredient is the **Annual Reset Provision**.

The annual reset provision is pretty simple. *Juror Number One*, earlier, we saw what it looks like if we are protected against market losses. But what if we could lock in our gains, too? That's what the annual reset provision does. Every year we have a positive gain, on the anniversary date of the policy, we lock in those gains and *that* becomes our new floor! We can never lose that money! The annual growth is ours to keep – forever, even if the market has a major downturn at some point in the future! Those locked-in gains can never be taken away from us! Does a 401(k) or IRA guarantee our gains? (The answer is no.)

Evidence #8 – the annual reset provision

So far, we've seen eight pieces of evidence. Those pieces of evidence are beginning to paint a picture of this *Alternate Retirement Plan* and how it is different from other retirement vehicles available to us today. We can also cross four items off of our list. You remember the list, right? I told you that I was going to give you a product that would:

1. Capture market gains whenever they occur; **PROVEN!** [Evidence #4]

2. NEVER participate in market losses; **PROVEN!** [Evidence #6]

3. Lock in the money you earn each year, so you could never lose it; **PROVEN!** [Evidence #8]

4. Allow you to access your money, even your gains, tax free;

5. Allow you to access your money for any reason, at any time and at any age without penalty;

6. Allow you to keep your money invested for as long as you like without penalty;

7. Be protected if you're sued or involved in a lawsuit (depending on the laws of your state);

8. Provide a large, income-tax free, payment to the person of your choosing if you died prematurely; **PROVEN!** [Evidence #1]

9. Allow a portion to be accelerated for purposes of chronic illness, acting in the stead of long-term care (without charge until activated)

As I'm sure you've noticed, we've proven items number one through three and we've got item number four directly in our sights. That's the item you've been waiting for, right *Juror Number One*? You're in luck. That's the item I've really wanted to tell you about because it's so important, especially when we get to retirement age. Once we hit that magical time, retirement time, we typically don't have the same tax deductions and tax "write-offs" that we do during the accumulation years of our life. Our kids are gone, the house is paid for, so all of our retirement income from those other, usual sources, will be taxed at the current tax rate. Who knows what that tax rate will be?

I am dedicating the complete next chapter to prove that through this *Alternate Retirement Plan*, it is possible to draw income in retirement (or at any stage of life) completely tax-free!

CHAPTER 8
THE EVIDENCE (PART 2)

So, let's think about this a minute, *Juror Number One*. Play along as we hit the fast-forward button on your investing life. Let's imagine you've been investing in the *Alternate Retirement Plan* for 20 years. You've placed a lot of importance and money in this retirement vehicle and it has performed well for you. Now, as retirement draws near, there are two ways to access your money.

The first, and most straightforward way is to make a **withdrawal**. The basic way it works is like a bank. When you go to a bank and make a withdrawal from your savings account, what happens? You have access to everything you've deposited, tax-free. It's tax-free because you paid taxes on it before you placed it in the account. However, while the money was in the savings account, it was earning interest and you haven't paid taxes on that, yet. As you access the money that you earned off of your savings, you are required to pay taxes on it.

In the same way, when we get ready to access our retirement money from the *Alternate Retirement Plan*, we can also make a **withdrawal**. Just like going to a bank, reaching *directly* into your savings account and accessing your money, the insurance company reaches *directly* into your investment account and accesses your money for you. A short time after you make your request, you'll have a check in your hand. Any investment payments you've made for all those years will be returned to you upon request, tax-free (because you paid taxes on them before you invested), but all of the gains you've earned over the course of those 20 years will require that taxes be paid as you access them (because they grew tax-deferred inside the policy).

It looks like this: You pay in $10,000 over the course of time and the Index Universal Life policy earns another $10,000. You have a total of $20,000 in your investment account. You want to make a withdrawal of $12,000. The first $10,000 is given to you tax-free. However, taxes will be required to be paid, at your current tax rate, on the other $2000.

This is the most straightforward way to access your money, as a **withdrawal**, but it isn't the tax-free way to access your money. You may have noticed that I keep hitting the **bold** button, every time I mention **withdrawal**. That's because there is a second way to access funds for your retirement and I want to keep it separate from the **withdrawal** method. The second method is the most amazing provision of the *Alternate Retirement Plan*. It's called the **loan** method.

The second objection…

"Objection! I object!! LOAN METHOD?? A loan is NO WAY to fund retirement!! I'm NOT taking out any loans when I get to that age!! I've worked my whole life to PAY OFF my loans! I'm not taking on any NEW loans! I'm not going to leave debts for my family to deal with when I die!! Get out of here!"

Juror Number One, cut me some slack! Hopefully over the course of the time we've had together, you've come to know me a little. You should probably realize, like a good magician, I've got a card up my sleeve. *[The judge says he will give me some leeway and has overruled the objection, but he says to make it good. I agreed.]*

What if I told you that you could take out a **loan**, pay **zero** interest on it and not have to pay it back? What if I told you that you were automatically approved, no matter what? Would that change your mind? I thought it might.

Let's talk about loans in general, for a moment. When you take out a loan (from a bank or an individual), there are no taxes paid on that loaned money. That's because the government doesn't consider it "earned" income. They know, at some point in the future, it will be repaid. There is interest charged on loans, but there are no taxes on loans.

Now, the second way to access money from the *Alternate Retirement Plan* is through a policy **loan**. This policy **loan** provision works in a very unique and beautiful way. To show how it works, let's contrast it with the first method (**withdrawal** method) of accessing our money. In our first method, we **withdraw** our money *straight from our investment account* inside our IUL. In the second method (**loan** method) we *don't touch our investment account* at all. We simply take a **loan** directly from the insurance company. The insurance company acts in the place of a bank and we borrow money from them. As policy owners, we never touch the money inside of our policy and because we don't, we don't have to pay taxes on it. We take a **loan** from the insurance company "bank," and as we've already established, there are no taxes on loans.

I can already see the wheels spinning right now, *Juror Number One*. You're about to ask, *"Why would the insurance company guarantee me a loan? Why would they not make me pay it back? How can they do this without charging me interest?"* Just hold your horses! I'm getting there.

I told you, in this **loan** method, that WE, as policy owners, never touch the money inside our investment account. We get a loan from the insurance company "bank." But, that doesn't mean the money in our account is never touched. The insurance company actually removes the same amount of money that was loaned to you out of your account, and places it in a different, interest-earning account. The insurance company uses *your money* as collateral for *your **loan***! Your money is your collateral!

Not only that, but since the money is already there, in your investment account, you are guaranteed approval from the insurance company for the **loan**! Guaranteed approval!

What's even better than that is the fact that since they have your money as collateral, the insurance company's not really concerned whether you pay back the **loan**. And what could be even better than that? Well, the insurance company is charging you interest on your **loan** – otherwise, it wouldn't be considered a **loan**, it would be a payment and therefore taxable as earned income. I told you, though, that when the insurance company gave you the **loan**, they used your money as collateral and placed it in an interest earning account, remember? The insurance company charges you the same interest rate on your **loan** as your collateral money is earning in its new account. So, you're charged interest, but your collateral money that is earning interest, covers what you're charged. It's a wash!

Since it's a **loan** and not a **withdrawal**, it is non-existent in the IRS's eyes. No taxes to be paid on the loan because the IRS can't see the "income" from the policy.

No taxes because it's a **loan**. *Guaranteed approval* on the **loan**. *No need to repay* the **loan**. *No interest paid* on the **loan**. *Invisible in the Internal Revenue Service's* eyes because it's a **loan**. And, 100% legal. How does all that sound?

Evidence #9 – tax-free access to cash

Do you know one other benefit to accessing your money through the **loan** method in retirement? You know you don't have to wait until retirement, right? You can take out a loan any time you have money in the account. But right now, let's talk specifically for when you access the money through the **loan** method at retirement age.

By the time you get to retirement, you've probably worked your whole life and paid an extraordinary amount of money into Social Security. If our politicians haven't found a way to keep that money for themselves by the time you get to retirement, at some point, you will start receiving your benefits, your monthly payments from the government. This Social Security Benefit is meant to complement your income, not be your only source.

From page 13 of the booklet *Social Security, Understanding the Benefits* which you can find on the Social Security Administration website:

> "Some people who get Social Security will have to **pay taxes on their benefits**. About 40 percent of our current beneficiaries **pay taxes on their benefits**. You'll have to **pay taxes on your benefits** if you file a federal tax return as an "individual" and your total income is more than $25,000. If you file a joint return, you'll have to **pay taxes** if you and your spouse have a total income that is more than $32,000."[1]

Do you see that? If you make more than $25,000 or $32,000 depending on your marital status, you'll be forced to **pay taxes** on your Social Security Benefits. You realize that's your money, that you paid into the fund and now that you want to access it, the government is taxing your benefits, right? Stinks, doesn't it?

So, I asked if you knew one other benefit to accessing your money through the **loan** method in retirement? Here it is: the *Alternate Retirement Plan* is invisible to the government and therefore doesn't create a taxation of your Social Security benefits. You're only taxed on your Social Security benefits if your **income** from other sources is more than $25,000 or $32,000. You could receive $100,000 from the *Alternate Retirement Plan* and because it is a **loan**, *not income*, it is invisible and will not cause your Social Security benefits to be taxed. At all. None. Zip. Zero. Nada.

Evidence #10 – will not cause Social Security benefits to be taxed

[1] https://www.ssa.gov/pubs/EN-05-10024.pdf

CHAPTER 9

THE EVIDENCE (PART 3)

The next several pieces of evidence proving that the *Alternate Retirement Plan* (aka the Index Universal Life policy) is the most incredible, fantastic, money-making, money-retaining, retirement plan available today, address the freedom you have in the *Plan* by contrasting it with the limitations that are imposed on other types of retirement vehicles. Buckle your seatbelt and hold on tight!

Let's see some of the limitations placed on OTHER retirement plans (traditional 401k, IRA, SIMPLE, SEP, etc.). According to the Internal Revenue Service website, IRS.gov:

"You cannot keep retirement funds in your account indefinitely. You generally have to

start taking withdrawals from your IRA,
SIMPLE IRA, SEP IRA, or retirement plan
account when you reach age 70½."

The government *forces* you to withdraw your
money from your traditional 401(k), IRA, SIMPLE,
SEP, etc., at age 70½ so they can begin to collect all
of the taxes you deferred since you set up the
account. Even if you don't need or want the money,
you are forced to withdraw it from your account.
Did you catch that? The government **FORCES**
you to begin taking withdrawals. Those forced
withdrawals are called Required Minimum
Distributions (RMDs). After the government forces
you to withdraw your money whether you want to
or not, they require you to pay taxes on the money
as well.

Guess what else happens with these plans, the
traditional 401(k), IRA, SIMPLE, SEP, etc. At age
70½, you are prohibited from adding any more
money to your investment. You're locked out of
your own account. So, the government is forcing
you to withdraw money whether you need it or not
and they are barring you from investing any
additional money. Why? Because they can… and
they want your tax money.

The *Alternate Retirement Plan* allows you to invest
your money for as long as you like without penalty.
If you don't need your money, leave it there. There
are no Required Minimum Distributions. If you

want to invest money into your 70s, 80s or 90s, go for it! There is no law or rule that says you can't.

Evidence #11 – no required minimum distributions (RMDs)

Evidence #12 – invest for as long as you like

Objection number three…

Here it comes: *"Objection! I happen to know that there are NO Minimum Required Distributions with certain other plans, like a Roth IRA. Top that, Mr. Fancy-Pants Lawyer! Maybe the Roth IRA is the best retirement plan available. I mean, the government even gives some tax breaks on it!"*

Well, *Juror Number One*, you're absolutely correct. The Roth IRA doesn't have RMDs and the government does treat the Roth IRA favorably when it comes to taxes. Do you know how the Roth IRA, really works, though? Explaining the nuances of the Roth IRA might help prove the *Alternate Retirement Plan* is a *better* plan.

How much money are you allowed to invest in a Roth IRA per year? In 2016, when I am writing this book, if you are under 50 years old, you're only allowed to invest $5500 a year. If you are over 50, you're allowed to invest $6500 a year. But what if you have more or want to invest more than that? Well, to put it gently: Tough.

How much are you allowed to invest each year in the *Alternate Retirement Plan*? The sky is the limit, that's how much. Nobody is going to tell you how much you can invest. If you've got an extra $20,000, BOOM! Invest it! Now, there is a certain way you have to do it, but it is easy to be done and the government allows it.

Evidence #13 – ability to invest more money

When can you access your money if it's invested in a Roth IRA? You can access any money that you invested at any point, much like a savings account, BUT if you access any of the gains you've earned before age 59½, you'll be required to pay taxes AND an early withdrawal penalty. Let me repeat that for you: TAXES and PENALTIES on **YOUR** money. That doesn't seem fair, does it? It's yours. Why should you have to pay penalties to access *your* money whenever you want it?

Guess what retirement plan doesn't require you to pay taxes OR penalties when you access your money (if done correctly)? That's right *Juror Number One*, the *Alternate Retirement Plan*, the Index Universal Life policy. No penalties or taxes for early withdrawals meaning you can access your money at any age!

Evidence #14 – no penalties for early withdrawals

You make too much money...

What happens if you make over $132,000 (in 2016) a year, as an investor filing taxes as 'single'? Well, that means you make too much money for the government to allow you to have a Roth IRA. Did you know that?

What's that you say? You're not filing as 'single'? You're married, filing jointly? Well, you have a limit of $194,000 in income. If you make a dollar more than that, you're no longer eligible for a Roth IRA. That stinks, doesn't it?

I've got great news for you! The *Alternate Retirement Plan* doesn't have income limits!! You can make as much as possible, single or filing jointly, it doesn't matter. You can make millions and still be eligible for this retirement plan. Why do you think 85% of the CEOs of Fortune 500 companies utilize this plan? Because it doesn't matter how much money they make, they're not penalized for it.

Evidence #15 – no income limits

What about this? What happens if you've been paying into your Roth IRA for 30 years and before you access a penny of your money, you accidentally step in the path of a rhinoceros that had recently escaped the zoo and you are trampled to death? The money in your Roth IRA goes to your beneficiaries – who then, wait for it, are required to pay income tax on that money. It was tax deferred, and now that they are accessing it, they will be forced to pay the taxes on it.

In the *Alternate Retirement Plan*, if you were swallowed by a shark, fell out of an airplane without a parachute, or jumped in front of a charging rhino, your beneficiaries would get the death benefit from the life policy AND also the gains from your investment portion in the policy! And, it would all be income tax free!

Evidence #16 – gains given to beneficiaries income-tax free

The judge leans over and suggests you think very carefully before you object again. *"Overruled!"*

[I know it looks like I singled out the Roth IRA and took a metaphorical baseball bat to it. That was completely unintentional. The Roth IRA is a pretty good retirement vehicle, but it does have a lot of limitations. All 'normal' retirement vehicles do. The Roth IRA was just the example I used to prove how much more versatile the Index Universal Life policy is. I could have just as easily "made my case" by using one of the other examples.]

CHAPTER 10
WRAPPING UP THE EVIDENCE

Let's look at our to-do list and see how we're progressing through these items:

I told you that I was going to give you a product that would:

1. Capture market gains whenever they occur; **PROVEN!** [Evidence #4]

2. NEVER participate in market losses; **PROVEN!** [Evidence #6]

3. Lock in the money you earn each year, so you could never lose it; **PROVEN!** [Evidence #8]

4. Allow you to access your money, even your gains, tax free; **PROVEN!** [Evidence #9]

5. Allow you to access your money for any reason, at any time and at any age without penalty; **PROVEN!** [Evidence #11, #14]
6. Allow you to keep your money invested for as long as you like without penalty; **PROVEN!** [Evidence #12]
7. Be protected if you're sued or involved in a lawsuit (depending on the laws of your state);
8. Provide a large, income-tax free, payment to the person of your choosing if you died prematurely; **PROVEN!** [Evidence #1]
9. Allow a portion to be accelerated for purposes of chronic illness, acting in the stead of long-term care (without charge until activated)

Wow. We've almost made our way through the entire list and we've proven some additional things that weren't on the list. I hope you're beginning to see how incredible the *Alternate Retirement Plan* actually is.

The next piece of evidence that I have to offer to you today is legal in nature – and when I say that, I mean outside of *our* "court" case. This is an *actual* legal piece of evidence that helps prove how awesome the *Alternate Retirement Plan* is. This piece of evidence is dependent on which state you live in, **so be sure and check your local laws**.

Crash. Boom. Flip.

Do you have any idea what could happen if you were involved in an accident that was your fault? I don't want to scare you, but let's play worst-case scenario here for a moment: You are driving on the freeway and you look down to change the radio station. Your car drifts ever so slightly and you end up clipping the rear bumper of the car in the lane next to you. When that happens the car goes into a spin and ends up rolling over, flipping over and over and over. Traffic on the freeway comes to a stop. You run over to the car, which has landed on its roof and you pull the unconscious driver out and to safety. You get out your cell phone and call an ambulance and the police.

Over the next few days, you begin to realize how this accident will affect you. You find out that the driver will live, but she will walk with a limp for the rest of her life. Not only will she live with a limp, but she was also a potential Olympic athlete that just had her life's dream taken away from her. After months and months in the hospital and rehab, she decides to take you to court, to sue you for more money than your car insurance carrier is legally obligated to pay. Now what happens?

If the court finds in favor of the plaintiff (and they will), you've got a big, expensive problem. All of your assets are accessible by the court. Can the court garnish your wages? Yes. But that's just the tip of the iceberg. You know that IRA, 401(k), etc., you've been investing in since you were 16 years old? The court has access to it. Overnight, all of your money and all of your retirement savings are gone. Goodbye.

A sigh of relief…

And then you remember what the court doesn't have access to. That's absolutely right. You remember you started an *Alternate Retirement Plan* twenty years ago and the court doesn't have access to your Index Universal Life Insurance policy. The courts see it solely as a life insurance policy and not an investment vehicle; therefore any excess money that is in the investment portion of the policy is protected from lawsuits.

Evidence #16 – protection from lawsuits

The final piece…

So here it is, we've come to it, the final piece of evidence that I will explain today in our case to prove that the *Alternate Retirement Plan*, the Index Universal Life policy, is the most incredible, fantastic, money-making, money-retaining, retirement plan available today. Just between you and me, *Juror Number One*, this is one of the most important and unique pieces of the *Alternate Retirement Plan*. Before I get to this last piece of evidence I'd like to revisit someone I spoke about earlier in this case, my cousin Joel. You remember my cousin Joel, don't you? He's the one with the go-to phrase, "If it sounds too good to be true, it *probably* is."

I want to tell you about what he is dealing with at this moment. His father, my uncle, has been diagnosed with Alzheimer's disease. He is 73 years old, and they found him this weekend, on the floor in the bathroom of his house, pinned between the toilet and the wall, completely immobile. This is just one in a series of events that has led the family to make some tough decisions. The family has realized they need to place him in a specialized Alzheimer's care facility.

Why do I begin our final piece of evidence by talking about my cousin Joel? This final piece of evidence has to do with accelerating a portion of your *Alternate Retirement Plan* for purposes of chronic illness, acting in the stead of long-term care.

I don't know about you, but when I hear the phrase, "Long Term Care," all I really hear is "Wallet Will Suffer." Now, whether that is justified or not is irrelevant. That's what I hear. When I hear the phrase "Long Term Care Insurance," all I hear is "Wallet Will Suffer More."

Take it from someone who is seeing it first hand, a family member needing Long Term Care is a very real possibility. According to recent statistics, there were 9 million Americans over the age of 65 who needed long-term care in 2012 and the number is estimated to rise to 12 million Americans who will need long term care in 2020. And, trust me, Long Term Care isn't cheap and neither is Long Term Care Insurance. The average cost for a Long Term Care facility is $73,000. That's *per year*. Depending where you are, (like New York $162,425), it can be much, much more expensive. The average cost of Long Term Care insurance is between $3,000 and $6,000 depending on your age and health, *per year*... and that's if you can even get the insurance to begin with. [1]

Let me explain how Long Term Care Insurance, generally, works. You apply for the insurance. Depending on your age, gender and health, you are either approved or declined for the insurance. If you're approved, you are charged a premium for the insurance – the older you are, the more expensive it is. On top of that, at any point, the insurance company can raise your rates. If you become disabled and in need of the insurance, you typically have to get a doctor to determine that you can no longer perform two of the six daily living activities without help. Those activities generally include: being able to eat without assistance, bathe, dress, use the toilet, walk and continence (holding back bodily functions).

Here's the drawback to Long Term Care Insurance: what if you don't need it? What if you never use it?

What happens to those thousands and thousands of dollars you've spent over the course of 20 or more years? You already know the answer, don't you, *Juror Number One*? All of the money is lost, spent, paid, gone.

That's where our final piece of evidence comes in. With the Index Universal Life policy, insurance companies have found a way to provide Long Term Care if it's ever needed, but they don't have to charge the client if it's never used. Sounds pretty good, doesn't it? Let me explain how it works in very general terms. Each insurance company has its own way of handling this, so be sure you know how your company deals with the Long Term Care Insurance *benefit (rider)* of the Index Universal Life policy.

A horse is a horse, of course, of course...

The *benefit* (called a *rider*) is simply added on top of the life policy. If the life policy was a horse, the *benefit* is a saddle sitting on top, waiting to be used. If you become disabled and a doctor says you fall into the category of needing Long Term Care, you sit in the saddle, using the benefit, to fulfill your needs.

There are two *general* ways companies handle the Long Term Care benefit in an Index Universal Life policy. We are not going to focus on the first method, but I should mention it. With this method, you are required to pay an additional charge each month to add the benefit to your policy. In other words, you are paying to save your spot in the saddle, in case you ever need to sit down. What that actually does is leave less money to be placed in the investment portion of your retirement plan. To me, that's not the best option. The best option is spelled F-R-E-E.

Method number two is a FREE benefit placed on the life insurance policy. It doesn't cost you anything until the day you activate it, the day you sit down in the saddle on the horse. If you need to activate the benefit, you only pay for the time you're actually using the benefit. You're only paying for the time you're actually sitting in the saddle. The beautiful thing is, if you never have to activate the benefit, if you never have to sit down in the saddle, you haven't wasted all of that money, paying for something you never used.

The way this Long Term Care benefit works is pretty simple. If you are deemed by a doctor to be in need of Long Term Care because you are unable to perform two of these functions without assistance, bathe, dress, use the toilet, walk and continence (holding back bodily functions), you can then activate the benefit on the policy. The insurance company will then distribute a portion of your death benefit to you early to use towards your Long Term Care needs. Typically, life insurance companies offer to pay you up to 2% of your death benefit on a monthly basis for a set period of time (like 4 years).

Here's a typical example: If you have a death benefit of $500,000 and activate your Long Term Care benefit, you'll typically have access to $10,000 a month maximum. You are not required to take the maximum.

$500,000
x 2%
 = $10,000

However, there is a catch! I told you this benefit is FREE **until activated**. The insurance company hasn't charged you for the benefit until you activated it, and now that you have, the company is going to get paid for providing the Long Term Care. They call it *discounting*.

So, let me explain *discounting* to you. As I mentioned, *discounting* is how you pay for the Long Term Care in the event you need it. In our example above, you are advanced 2% of your death benefit on a monthly basis. To pay for the benefit, the insurance company then takes a payment from that monthly amount. They *discount* the amount that is paid to you. "The discount usually works as follows: convert your age to a percentage, and then apply it to the monthly amount…"[2]

If you are 80 years old, and we convert that to a percentage, that would be 80%. Multiply the 80%

by our $10,000 monthly amount and we end up with $8,000 a month in benefit.

$10,000
x 80%
= $8,000 monthly amount available

The $8,000 is the maximum monthly allotment, but you do not have to use the maximum amount. And as a reminder, you don't have to use this benefit if you don't need it and you're not charged unless you activate it.

Evidence #17 – long-term care benefit rider that is free until activated

With that final piece of evidence, I would like to rest my case that the *Alternate Retirement Plan* is the most incredible, fantastic, money-making, money-retaining, retirement plan available today.

I told you that I was going to give you a product that would:
1. Capture market gains whenever they occur; **PROVEN!** [Evidence #4]
2. NEVER participate in market losses; **PROVEN!** [Evidence #6]
3. Lock in the money you earn each year, so you could never lose it; **PROVEN!** [Evidence #8]
4. Allow you to access your money, even your gains, tax free; **PROVEN!** [Evidence #9]

5. Allow you to access your money for any reason, at any time and at any age without penalty; **PROVEN!** [Evidence #11, #14]

6. Allow you to keep your money invested for as long as you like without penalty; **PROVEN!** [Evidence #12]

7. Be protected if you're sued or involved in a lawsuit (depending on the laws of your state); **PROVEN!** [Evidence #16]

8. Provide a large, income-tax free, payment to the person of your choosing if you died prematurely; **PROVEN!** [Evidence #1]

9. Allow a portion to be accelerated for purposes of chronic illness, acting in the stead of long-term care (without charge until activated) **PROVEN!** [Evidence #17]

… and I feel that I have done that. I have proven my nine points (and then some) through seventeen pieces of evidence.

There are a couple things you absolutely need to know (circumstantial evidence) about the *Alternate Retirement Plan* that I would like to mention, so that you will have a complete picture of the retirement vehicle. You will be able to make a completely informed decision, and then it will be up to you, *Juror Number One*, to decide.

[1] All stats taken from the article:
40 Must-Know Statistics About Long-Term Care
http://news.morningstar.com/articlenet/article.aspx?id=564139

[2]*Look Before You LIRP*, McKnight, page 48.

CHAPTER 11
CIRCUMSTANTIAL EVIDENCE

There are a handful of very important things to remember if you're looking at the *Alternate Retirement Plan* as one of your retirement vehicles. Most of them are no big deal in my estimation, just things to be aware of, but the last one looks a little scary on the surface.

That's life (insurance)...

Item A: This is a life insurance product with an attached investment account. In *my* educated opinion, it is the best investment account available today for the *right* client. **However, at its core, this is a life insurance policy and every monthly payment made is not only used for investment purposes, but will be used to purchase a month's worth of life insurance and pay administrative fees.** What this means is if you have a certain amount of money to invest each month, part of your capital will be spent to purchase life insurance and only the remainder will be used toward the investment.

Let's say you have allocated $500 a month to use toward your retirement. If you invest in a mutual fund or IRA, since there is no life insurance to purchase, and you are only charged the basic administration fees, more of that initial $500 will be used toward the investment. In the Index Universal Life policy, the amount that will be used toward the investment is potentially less because the first portion is used to purchase life insurance and also pay fees.

However, I don't think this is a big deal. The *Alternate Retirement Plan,* using life insurance as a retirement vehicle, has "been called a 'scam' by many in the financial advice industry. The first complaint often levied against it is the relatively high fees associated with policies. But a properly structured [*Alternate Retirement Plan*] can dilute the effect of fees by aggressively overfunding the policy."[1] In other words, if you structure your policy correctly, the way that has been outlined in this court case, the *Alternate Retirement Plan's* fees are a non-issue.

"Fred Reish, an employee benefits lawyer, says it is not uncommon for fees on a small 401(k) plan to break down like this: 0.25% a year for the plan adviser, 0.25% a year for the record keeper and 0.75% a year for mutual funds, totaling 1.25%."[2] So, when we compare the fees between the two plans, the *Alternate Retirement Plan* and the 401(k), "the expenses within the [*Alternate Retirement Plan*] can cost as little as 1% of the annual account balance over the life of the program. And, that's less than the average annual expenses in the typical 401(k)."[3] Moral of the story: *the fees are basically a wash, but you have to decide if the upsides to the IUL outweigh the fact you potentially aren't investing as much each month as you could in some other investment vehicle.* Do the pros outweigh the cons?

Item B: As we've talked about, this is an Index Universal Life policy with an attached investment account. We can access tax-free money, through the policy **loan** method. It's tax-free because it's a **loan**. If this doesn't seem familiar, it's because you skipped some pages in the book! Go back and read Chapter Eight.

As we've seen, the government doesn't consider the money as "income" because it is a **loan.**

However, if the policy cancels at any point while you have a loan outstanding, the loan changes to a withdrawal (of gains) and therefore will be seen as income by the government. It will then be considered a taxable event by the IRS. Moral of the story: *don't let your policy cancel if you have an outstanding loan.*

Item C: When you take that **loan** out, it will affect the death benefit of the life insurance. If you look back to page 70, I said *"we are able add additional money and to leave the money in the account. That additional money, the money you have invested and any gains, gets **added to your death benefit**. If you were to die, your beneficiary would receive the death benefit as well as everything you have invested and earned."* Once you start accessing the money either through the **loan** method or the **withdrawal** method, it will reduce the death benefit in proportion to the amount removed. Look at it this way, when you invest, you are adding to the death benefit. Because investing has caused the death benefit to increase, when you access the money, that will cause the death benefit to decrease. If you never access the money, your beneficiary gets that growth at the time of your death. Either you get the money while you're alive or your beneficiary gets it after you're gone.

Item D: The Index Universal Life policy is a 'cash-driven' policy. What that means is as long as there is cash in your investment portion of the life policy, even just $1, the policy will stay in force. **However, if you remove all of your money out of the investment portion of the retirement account, the policy will cancel.** Moral of the story: *don't remove 100% of your cash from your policy.* Your agent will be able to help with this. Listen to him or her!

Item E: Here's a cool benefit of this Index Universal Life being a 'cash-driven' policy. The policy will stay in force as long as there is cash in the investment portion and if there is cash in the investment portion, you're not required to add more to it. What that means is as long as there is cash in the investment portion of the policy, you don't necessarily have to make monthly payments. Remember, the cost of insurance and any fees will be removed from the cash value even if you're not making a monthly deposit. The good news is if there is enough money in the policy to pay the cost of insurance and fees, the policy will continue. You will continue to earn interest on any money still invested if the market rises and your *Alternate Retirement Plan* will stay in force. Admittedly, this is not a great way to grow your retirement income, but if you have an emergency and you need to stop making payments for a few months, that is an option with this policy – *as long as there is enough cash in the investment portion*. **However, if you remove all of your money out of the investment portion of the retirement account *or if the insurance and fees depletes the cash because you've stopped making monthly installments*, the policy will cancel.** Moral of the story: *continue to make monthly payments and if you stop, start again as soon as possible*. Always keep your agent in the loop because your agent will be able to help with this. Listen to him or her!

Item F: The IRS says that you can only invest a certain amount of money in a life policy. The amount you are able to invest is based on the face amount of the policy. The higher the face amount, the more you can invest. If you put more money into a life policy than the IRS allows, the IRS no longer views it as a life insurance policy. They view it as a Modified Endowment Contract (MEC). Once the IRS views it as a MEC, it is always viewed as a MEC. The simple way to prevent a life policy from becoming a MEC is to raise the face amount of the policy to be in line with the IRS standards.

The reason I'm even bringing this up is because there could potentially be tax problems if your *Alternate Retirement Plan* is viewed as a Modified Endowment Contract by the IRS. The problem with a life policy that has become a MEC occurs when you want to access any of the cash value in the policy. **If the policy is viewed as a MEC and you access the cash as a withdrawal or *even as a loan*, it becomes a taxable event.** That obviously hinders the "tax-free retirement" aspect of using life insurance as a retirement vehicle. Moral of the story: *work with a professional when you set this retirement plan in force to prevent it from becoming a Modified Endowment Contract.*

Item G: As we've seen from the section in Chapter Six, subtitled "How it works..." the insurance company uses bonds as our downside protection to guarantee our 0% floor. It takes a year for those bonds to mature, so for the first year, our investment money is "locked." We know that we will only make money and never lose money in this investment vehicle. **However, we can't track how much money we make during the first year.** If you are one of those people who has to look at your returns every day, you need to know going into it, you will not be able to have a *current* figure until after the first year. You can track the index (ex: the S&P 500) to see how it is performing, but not your returns.

On the surface...

This last item looks scary on the surface, but don't let it get to you. Once you understand it, I think you'll find it's not that big of a deal.

Item H: We've talked a lot about the cap and floor to this Index Universal Life policy; see Chapter Seven, evidence #4. In my examples, I used a cap of 12%. **However, the caps are not guaranteed and the insurance company can lower them at any point.** The insurance companies typically have a minimum cap guarantee – somewhere in the 2% -3% range. There are a couple reasons why I don't think we have to worry about the cap rates being lowered dramatically. The first reason is basic capitalism.

Basic capitalism states that if *Insurance Company A*

lowers their cap rate from 12% to 6% and *Insurance Company B* still offers a cap of 12%, we will all purchase our policies from *Insurance Company B*, right? It will **cost** *Insurance Company A* money to lower their cap. We know that insurance companies are in business to make money therefore we should think they are going to be hesitant to lower their caps.

The second reason I believe we need not worry about the insurance company lowering their cap is history. "Between 2000 and 2015, we saw stock market rates of return zig-zagging all over the board. If ever there were a testing ground for how index caps might respond to rough market conditions, that was it. Even in the wake of the 2008-2009 financial crisis, some IUL companies only lowered their cap by 1%! In short, for insurance companies to lower their caps to the point where we might begin to worry, the stock market would have to be *even more* volatile and unpredictable than it has been over the last 15 years."[4]

There is one more thing I would like to mention as we're talking about these caps. We have talked about insurance companies having the ability to lower the caps, but they also have the ability to raise the caps as well. If the economy is doing well, these caps could potentially be raised allowing each of us that have decided to use the *Alternate*

Retirement Plan as a retirement vehicle to capture even more market gains! Moral of the story: *you have to decide if the potential outlined in this type of retirement vehicle is worth the risk of the earning cap being movable.*

That's it. As far as I can tell, those are all of the things to be aware of when thinking about the *Alternate Retirement Plan* and the best ways to avoid any pitfalls. You should have a fair and balanced view of this amazing product. Is it right for everyone? No. *No* plan is right for everyone. The more important question is this – is this plan right for **you?**

[1]*Life Insurance Retirement Plans: Alternative or Rip-Off?* Robert Bloink and William H. Byrnes. http://www.thinkadvisor.com/2011/11/25/life-insurance-retirement-plans-alternative-or-rip?&slreturn=1473283816

[2]*"Are fees draining your 401(k) retirement savings?,"* Christine Dugas, *USA Today, Aug. 25, 2009.*

[3]*The Life Insurance Retirement Plan (LIRP) Advantage.* Scott Ho. http://www.financialsafetynet.org/retirement/life-insurance-retirement-plan-lirp-advantage/4637

[4]*Look Before You LIRP,* McKnight p.70

CHAPTER 12
CLOSING STATEMENTS

Juror Number One, at the beginning of this court case, I made a promise to you and I've kept that promise. I promised you a product that would:

1. Capture market gains whenever they occur;
2. NEVER participate in market losses;
3. Lock in the money you earn each year, so you could never lose it;
4. Allow you to access your money, even your gains, tax free;
5. Allow you to access your money for any reason, at any time and at any age without penalty;
6. Allow you to keep your money invested for as long as you like without penalty;

7. Be protected if you're sued or involved in a lawsuit (depending on the laws of your state);

8. Provide a large, income-tax free, payment to the person of your choosing if you died prematurely;

9. Allow a portion to be accelerated for purposes of chronic illness, acting in the stead of long-term care (without charge until activated)

I set out to prove that the *Alternate Retirement Plan* is the most incredible, fantastic, money-making, money-retaining, retirement plan available today. Here, in abbreviated form, are the different pieces of evidence I gave while trying to prove that point:

Evidence #1 – the death benefit

Evidence #2 – avoids probate

Evidence #3 – cash accumulation

Evidence #4 – room to grow

Evidence #5 – tax-deferred growth

Evidence #6 – protection against market losses

Evidence #7 – accurate return figures

Evidence #8 – the annual reset provision

Evidence #9 – tax-free access to cash

Evidence #10 – will not cause Social Security benefits to be taxed

Evidence #11 – no required minimum distributions (RMDs)

Evidence #12 – invest for as long as you like

Evidence #13 – ability to invest more money

Evidence #14 – no penalties for early
withdrawals

Evidence #15 – no income limits

Evidence #16 – protection from lawsuits

Evidence #17 – long-term care benefit rider that
is free until activated

Juror Number One, only you can know if the *Alternate Retirement Plan* is the right plan for you. What I've tried to do is give you an accurate representation of the many different aspects of this wonderful investment vehicle. It genuinely might not be the right one for you. Please, take some time, think about what you've read in this 'court case' and give some serious consideration to an Index Universal Life policy. My cousin Joel always says "If something seems too good to be true, it *probably* is," but I think he would add this phrase to it, "If something seems too good to be true, it *probably* is, unless it's the *Alternate Retirement Plan*!" Thank you, *Juror Number One,* for your time and attention today.

At this point, the judge leans over to you and instructs you to be honest, fair and truthful… with yourself. He says "Juror Number One, i*f you haven't taken the time to think about your retirement, it's not too late. Your retirement is very important. Please, take the first step and go see a professional about it. If you tell that professional you want a tax free retirement, an* Alternate Retirement Plan *or an Index Universal Life*

123

policy, and they don't know what you're talking about, give them a copy of this book and **go find a professional who does.**" The judge concludes his instructions to you and sends you out to deliberate.

As you leave, you hear the bailiff again boom, "All Rise!!" as the judge prepares to leave the courtroom.

For more information about the author,
to order additional books or request
information about speaking engagements, visit:
DavidPorterBooks.com

ABOUT THE AUTHOR

David Porter and his wife Lauren reside in
Birmingham, Alabama. David has multiple
college degrees and extensive post-graduate
training in insurance and financial services.
He is multi-licensed to sell insurance and financial
products and has worked in the industry for
over fifteen years. In the ever-changing world
of financial planning, David works diligently
through continuing education to remain
current on new products and services and has been
recognized as an industry leader through multiple
national and international honors.

All photos of the author courtesy of:
Kim Brantley Photography
www.kimbrantleyphotography.com

21693201R00075

Made in the USA
Columbia, SC
22 July 2018